Korean
Bhikkhunī

Korean Bhikkhunī : *The Hidden History of Female Buddhist Monks Illuminated*

Author	Ha Choon-Sang
Translator	Chun Ock-Bae
Photographer	Jang Myeong-Hwak
Publisher	International Cultural Foundation

Copyright © 2016 International Cultural Foundation
Publishing License 300-2016-42 registered on April 18, 2016

The International Cultural Foundation
42-9, Bukchon-ro, Jongno-gu, Seoul, Republic of Korea

Telephone	82-2-743-2089
Fax	82-2-763-1543
Homepage	www.icfkorea.com

Text © Ha Choon-Sang, 2018.
Translation © Chun Ock-Bae, 2018.
Photograph © Jang Myeong-Hwak, 2018.

ISBN   979-11-958119-2-2 03220 (paper)   979-11-958119-3-9 05220 (E-book)

Korean
Bhikkhunī

The Hidden History of Female Buddhist Monks Illuminated

Author Ha Choon-Sang
Translator Chun Ock-Bae
Photographer Jang Myeong-Hwak

There's no discrimination between *Bhikkhunīs* and *Bhikkhus*. There's only unfaltering practice!

The rediscovery of Korean culture and the history of *Bhikkhunīs* are rewritten.

 International Cultural Foundation (ICF)
Together We Can

Notes from the Publisher

International Cultural Foundation

50th Anniversary 2018

ICF Chairman
Chun Hong-Duk

Korean Bhikkhunī: The Hidden History of Female Buddhist Monks Illuminated

The International Cultural Foundation is a private organization founded in February 1968 by Chun Shin-Yong with the aim of introducing Korean culture to foreign countries and promoting international cultural exchange. Frustrated and disappointed by the lack of literature on Korean culture available at America's most prestigious university libraries when he visited in the 1960s, Mr. Chun returned home inspired to find a way to further global awareness and knowledge of his beloved and beautiful Korea, and this year now marks the 50th anniversary.

Half a century of collaborating with the most preeminent scholars and writers of Korean culture have yielded a catalog of over twenty books on varied subjects of interest both nationally and abroad. From the ICF's very inception, Dr. Yeo Seok-Ki, a beacon of Korean academia--former Director of the Korea Culture and Arts Foundation and of the American Culture Research Center at Korea University—partnered with Mr. Chun to ensure that only the most relevant and fascinating topics would be explored. Distinguished academics such as Dr. Kim Chan-Kyu of Kyung Hee University, former director of the Korean Society of International Law, Professor Kim Yeol-Kyu of Seogang University and Professor Seo Don-Gak of Seoul National University have since enthusiastically taken up the mantle in researching, editing, and penning our ongoing compendium of humble but sincere contributions to our efforts to inform the domestic and international academic communities. These publications, which began in 1970 when Korean traditional culture was almost unknown abroad, may now become more important than ever as Korea stands on the verge of achieving a level of global acceptance, recognition, renown, and popularity to a degree heretofore undreamt.

Each of these publications was written with the cooperation and synergy of several experts in each subject to provide a balanced and objective view of Korean culture. Some notable titles have been: *Humor in Korean Culture, Upper Class Culture in the Joseon Yi Dynasty Korea, Korean Folklore Culture, Culture of Korean Shamanism, The King's Secret Emissary in the Joseon Dynasty, Korean Geomancy [feng shui, pronounced poong su in Korean], Arirang Culture in Korea, and Korean Buddhist Culture*. Most of these books were published in English as well and then distributed to various research institutions including Korean and foreign libraries. Though every volume is obviously very informative and educational, the goal of the publication and the purpose of the individual books was never merely that of edification nor the perfunctory intent of the dissemination of Korean culture to other countries, but truly it was the unadulterated excitement at the possibility of being able to share all that is unique and wondrous about Korea with the whole world.

In May 1974, the International Cultural Foundation published *Korean Buddhist Culture* as the third publication of its Korean Culture Series and examined topics including the sculpture of the Silla Dynasty period (BC 57-AD 935), the printing culture of the Goryo Dynasty period (918-1392) and its seminal publication of volumes of Buddhist history, and the story of prominent Korean writer-poet monk Manhae Han Yong-un (1879-1944). Especially noteworthy is the life and thought of the illustrious Buddhist monk Wonhyo (617-686). In his philosophy of "One Mind", Wonhyo proposed a unified ideology to bring together and harmonize the differing ideological systems that had been struggling to co-exist during Korea's Three Kingdoms period (BC 18-AD 668).

Although in modern-day Korea, Christianity has long been the prevailing religion, just as in much of the rest of the world, Buddhism has such historical significance to Korean culture that it is absolutely embedded in and woven throughout the tapestry of Korean cultural identity in general and even arguably underlies every Korean's spiritual framework. Buddhist traditions have had a foothold in the history of Korea's formation and transformations for well over 1,600 years. Indeed, a huge portion of Korean historical national cultural treasures come down to us from the collected artworks of Silla's Buddhist culture (BC 57-AD 935), proudly displayed at the many museums, temples, and palaces throughout Seoul and South Korea. Thus, as the International Cultural

Foundation set out to celebrate its Golden Anniversary, it seemed only fair and fitting that the topic of Buddhist contributions to Korean society be revisited.

In this special anniversary edition, *Korean Bhikkhunī : The Hidden History of Female Buddhist Monks Illuminated*, the culture of Korean female Buddhist monks (*Bhikkhunīs*)— sometimes described by the more commonly understandable term "nuns"—is explored and elucidated. Just as integral as Buddhist tradition is to the history of Korea at large, so too is the existence and difficult history of *Bhikkhunīs* to the establishment and proliferation of that very culture.

Korean Bhikkhunī: The Hidden History of Female Buddhist Monks Illuminated presents a dynamic view of the history and current status of *Bhikkhunīs* and their invaluable contributions to Korean Buddhism since its first introduction to the Korean Peninsula in AD 372. It also introduces the relationships between and the processes of establishment for the various *Bhikkhunī* orders, focusing on the eleven existing *Bhikkhunī* orders in Korea. In the course of the development of traditional Korean society, women have generally been underappreciated and relegated to second-class citizenship, and the history of Buddhist orders, of course, is no exception. Nevertheless, it would not be an exaggeration to say that, if not for the unending self-sacrifice, tireless dedication, and devoted service of Korean *Bhikkhunī*s, Korean Buddhism simply would not have achieved the status it has today without them.

This English version of *Korean Bhikkhunī* is a translation of the Korean version, *Bhikkhunīs- Disciples of the Buddha*, first published by the International Cultural Foundation Press in June 2016 and written by Dr. Ha Choon-Sang, a professor at Dongguk University and noted authority on Korean *Bhikkhunī*s. The Korean version of this book has encouraged fresh discourse on Korean Buddhism, and, after a year in preparation, we hope now that this English edition will enable international readers to expand their awareness of Korean Buddhist culture as well. It is hoped that students of Korean Buddhist culture in English-speaking countries will gain a better understanding of the life and history of Korean *Bhikkhunī*s who facilitated and reinforced the development of Buddhist culture in Korea and who audaciously trailblazed for gender equality before even being aware of their own bravery.

As the International Cultural Foundation continues its important work of showcasing Korean culture academically to the rest of the world in the hopes of furthering global understanding in the digital era and contributing to an everlastingly peaceful planet, we commemorate the 50th anniversary of the ICF and renew our commitment to the ideals of the free exchange of culture and historical knowledge by making available digital versions of many of our past publications available on our website. We do this to make it easier for researchers, scholars and casual readers alike to study and better appreciate Korean culture. In addition, we hope that US soldiers and their families stationed in Korea will use our website to better understand the country in which they are living. In the effort to promote goodwill and good times and to help make life more enjoyable and interesting for American soldiers in Korea, the ICF also participates in organizing and supporting a variety of annual festivals around Korea, such as the Namwon Chunhyangje Festival, the Jinhae Gunhang Festival, the Cheongsong Apple Festival, and the Gimpo Boat Festival, as well as the annual USO Six Star Salute held in conjunction with the Eighth United States Army.

The publication of this English edition was made possible by the efforts of Mr. Chun Ock-Bae who, as the current Director of the Korea Institute of Buddhist English Translation (KIBET), contributes greatly to the globalization of Korean Buddhism. Director Chun helped create and continues to update and support the *Digital Dictionary of Buddhism*, along with Professor Charles Muller of Tokyo University. This online dictionary is also now available in printed form under the title *Korean-English Dictionary of Buddhism*. Director Chun graduated from Korea University Law School and studied Buddhism at Dongguk University.

Many thanks, of course, to Dr. Ha Choon-Sang of Dongguk University for writing this important and much-needed book. Dr. Ha is an expert on Korean *Bhikkhunīs*, a group that historically has always been marginalized and disparaged by traditionally male-dominated mainstream Korean Buddhism. This English version will be a very valuable resource for a better understanding of *Bhikkhunīs* and their history, not only here in Korea but around the world.

Mr. Jang Myeong-Hwak, a professional photographer, took all of the photographs used in this book. For the past 20 years he has lectured on photography at many college campuses and has a great deal of experience photographing Korean temples. He has worked on this book with great enthusiasm and attentiveness for the past five months.

Sincere gratitude to all others who helped make this publication possible, with special thanks to the following: Director of Operations, Mr. Kim Eui-Han; Advertising Director, Mr. Jeon Hyeong-Ki; and President of the *Gimpo Journal*, Mr. Kwak Jong-Kyu.

It is the sincere hope of the International Cultural Foundation that this book will contribute to fostering and promoting a deeper and more comprehensive understanding of Korean culture worldwide and prove to be a very beneficial resource and springboard for further research into Korean Buddhism.

And, as always, thank you so much for learning, sharing, and celebrating our world with us!

Author's Comments

"Practitioners on the Buddhist path, when the morning sun comes up, the first sign that appears in the sky is the reddish dawn.

Likewise, there are pioneers in practicing the Noble Eightfold Path, and there are forerunners, and they are good friends.

My attendants, if you're a practitioner with such a good friend, you can expect to finally learn and refine the Noble Eightfold Path."

- Samyutta Nikāya 45:49

I love this verse spoken by the Buddha, and I would not hesitate to choose it as my favorite if I could only choose one. Here, the Buddha is saying that a good friend (*kalyāṇamitta* 善友 a virtuous friend) may become the precursor to one's wisdom. The Noble Eightfold Path is the sacred road to enlightenment (涅槃, *Nibbāna*); it is also a virtuous friend that can keep you on the holy path.

Quoting the Buddha in the *Suttanipāta* 1:3 「*The Rhinoceros-horn*」 11:

"If you encounter a compassionate companion or a mature friend, you will be able to overcome any difficulties and find happiness. Go with him." Here, the Buddha is referring to the *saṅgha* (Buddhist order) and saying that a person not in harmony with the Noble Eightfold Path cannot be a good friend.

The Buddha goes on to say in the same scripture, *Suttanipāta* 1:3 「*The Rhinoceros-horn*」 12:

"If you do not find a mature and dynamic partner, a mature friend, then, like a king abandoning his conquered kingdom, go alone like the horn of a rhinoceros."

This book is about such good, virtuous friends. They are *Bhikkhunīs* (Buddhist nuns) on the Noble Eightfold Path who strive to expunge all inner desires, obsessions and defilements, and yet we know little about them. Deep-rooted bias against women in Korea's history prevented many of their achievements from being recorded, but on the other hand, they never sought fame and glory. I see them as unsung heroes. Many outsiders and non-Buddhists thought *Bhikkhunīs* were only trying to escape reality and looked at them with curious, pathetic eyes. But a *Bhikkhunī* is a special sort of person.

In writing this book, *Korean Bhikkhunī: The Hidden History of Female Buddhist Monks Illuminated*, I have three objectives in mind. The first is to increase public understanding of *Bhikkhunīs* and their pursuit of the highest cause: to become enlightened and save sentient beings from suffering. The traditional perception of *Bhikkhunīs* has been misunderstood or distorted to some extent over the years. In the past, novels, movies and dramas about *Bhikkhunīs* were often adapted into sensational, secular stories. It is only recently that the public's understanding has begun to change. It is now more and more accepted that women should be allowed to make their own autonomous decisions to achieve happiness and self-fulfillment.

Five years ago a movie directed by Chang-jae Lee debuted in Korea titled On the Road. It documents the lives of different *Bhikkhunīs* from all walks of life every day for one year. What follows is a brief description of some of them:

One young lady had graduated from a prestigious American university. She became a *Bhikkhunī* after practicing at a Zen center. One young woman came to the temple to become a *Bhikkhunī* after researching the subject on the internet. One young lady was sent to live at a temple when she was a child. Later she became a *Bhikkhunī.* One middle-aged *Bhikkhunī* said she had two children, and her husband was a manager in a large corporation. After receiving her family's permission, she became a nun at the age of 49. One older lady had been a *Bhikkhunī* for 37 years. She became one after her mother convinced her that this world was a "sea of suffering" and she should go live in a temple. Each woman in the movie has her own story to tell. They are not escapists or avoiding reality. They are struggling for personal fulfillment. They are sacrificing their wants and desires to search for inner peace. We should honor and respect them.

My second objective is to increase awareness of gender discrimination. A *Bhikkhunī* is a Buddhist practitioner who should be considered the equal of any *Bhikkhu* (male ordained monk). When some *Bhikkhunīs* first encounter the *Eight Precepts Specifically for Bhikkhunīs* and 'the five theories on the impossibility of women's enlightenment', they are apt to be frustrated and possibly angered at the obvious sexual discrimination. Why should they be victims of sexual discrimination?

In the context of history, what is our perception of a *Bhikkhunī*? I asked that question earlier in several previous articles. I hope the future of Korean Buddhism can be realized in the dynamism and life-force of Korean *Bhikkhunīs* who hopefully will usher in a new era of practice, education, social welfare and culture. We must recognize and address the irrationality of some practices by Buddhist orders that only perpetuate gender discrimination.

My third objective is to shed light on the fact that the status of *Bhikkhunīs* is now established. Evidence of this is the election of a *Bhikkhunī* as a chairperson in the Jogye Order of Korean Buddhism. However, all candidates in the 10th (October 17, 2011) and the 11th (October 12, 2015) elections, in their official commitment presentations, promised in vain to try and increase the number of *Bhikkhunīs* holding positions in the Jogye Order's Central Congress. Therefore, there is still more work to be done.

The number of monks in the Jogye Order is about 13,000, and the number of *Bhikkhunīs* is about half that. Of Korea's

2,500 Buddhist temples, about 1,000 are *Bhikkhunī* temples. These statistics clearly show a bias in favor of male monks. So what should we do? My answer to that is in my book.

This book is endowed with the direct and indirect grace of many wise people around me. First of all, the Buddha's words, which greatly helped in the flow of the text, came from the *Pāli-Nikāya*, which was translated and published by the Chogi Buljeon Yeonguwon (初期佛典研究員, Korea Institute of Early Faith and Korea Pāli Temple Association) in which Ven. Gakmook, Ven. *Bhikkhunī* Daelim, Dr. Jeon Jae-sung and Ven *Bhikkhunī*. Il-a are some of the key players. I also received advice from Ven. *Bhikkhunī* Seonil (abbot of *Dhammarang* Temple in Yongin) and my wife, Hwayeon Buddhist painter (佛母). I also reviewed many writings and inscriptions on the history of temples and historical monuments as part of the "Korean Culture" series. There aren't enough words to express my gratitude to Chairman Chun Hong-duk and Executive Director of Operation Kim Eui-han of the International Cultural Foundation for Culture. I also give sincere thanks to my photographer and friend Jang Myeong-hwak whose skill greatly elevated the quality of this book. And lastly, I would like to express my gratitude to all of you on the path to enlightenment.

In the middle of Autumn, 2018

Wooseong (宇晟) *Ha Choon-sang*

Table of Contents

IV. The Activities of *Bhikkhunīs* in Korea Today

V. The Korean *Bhikkhunī Dhamma* Family Today

Glossary

❶

What is a *Bhikkhunī* (Buddhist nun)?

1.
Renouncing Secular Life to Become a Monk

It ruins your spirit, poor old man.
Age makes beauty wither,
In all its fascinating forms.
Your life breaks into pieces.
Even if you live to be a hundred,
The last stop is death.
Death is inevitable,
It destroys everything.

- Saṃyutta Nikāya 48:41

If anyone asks, "Which is more certain, life or death?", most people would reply that death is more certain. Still, people act as though they will live forever. This is a tragic illusion. Old age, sickness and death are inevitable, though not necessarily in that order. In Buddhism, birth, aging, sickness, and death are referred to as the "four afflictions" (四苦), and they are the destiny of all people.

Renunciation, where are we going?

One day, a young man told his father,

"If I could not die, if illness could not damage my health, if age could not destroy my youth, and if misery could not destroy my happiness, I would not renounce secular life to become a monk." (*Buddhacarita Chapter* 5)

The father chided him, "Do not even think about such things", warning that it was foolishness to become a monk. Perhaps most parents would respond similarly if their own son or daughter expressed a desire to become a monk for these reasons. That is because we know birth, old age, sickness and death are inevitable and cannot be avoided.

However, the young man replied that, if he must confront these four afflictions, he would prefer to abandon secular life and become a monk in hopes of confronting and overcoming them. Eventually, the young man left behind all his worldly distractions. He became a wandering ascetic and concentrated his full energies on pursuing a spiritual path. This young ascetic was Siddhattha Gotama, a prince of the Sakya Kingdom who was destined to become the "Buddha." His father was King Suddhodana of the Sakya Kingdom regarded as a 'descendant of Sun'.

This story explains the fundamental background of why the Buddha renounced secular life and became a monk to attain enlightenment. It can also be understood through the Buddha's own confession in later years, "If there were not three of these sufferings (aging and sickness and death), I would not have appeared in this world."

There is another story of the latter years of the Buddha. One day, Ānanda, one of his ten major disciples, rubbed the Buddha's hands and feet while they sat in the sun and said:

> "It is wonderful, venerable sir! It is amazing, venerable sir! The Blessed One's complexion is no longer pure and bright, his limbs are all flaccid and wrinkled, his body is stooped, and some alteration is seen in his faculties—in the eye faculty, the ear faculty, the nose faculty, the tongue faculty, the body faculty."

> *- Samyutta Nikāya* 48:41

Ānanda thought that Buddha would never die or be sick. The Buddha then explained that all young men will eventually become old and all healthy men will become sick. Seeing Ananda's frustration, Buddha explained to him kindly the way an old man would explain to his grandson. "I am getting old and unhealthy like everybody else. Eventually, I will be dead."It is a sort of confession to admit that it is inevitable for all men to be born and die. Even if one is free of all troubles, is released from all desires and obsessions, and becomes an enlightened Buddha, one cannot escape sickness, aging and death. That is the way of this world. All things of this world eventually cease to be.

So the last teaching of the Buddha is that there is no other way but to devote oneself diligently to seeking enlightenment. Of course, rigorous self-discipline and practice aim to realize the true value of life and to abandon all greed, obsession and suffering. Buddhism teaches, "Seek enlightenment above to transform sentient beings below (上求菩提下化衆生)." This means one must first attain enlightenment through self-cultivation and then save all sentient beings. This is the sacred duty of a *Bodhisatta*. The ultimate goal of every Buddhist practitioner should be to lead a clean life and to overcome all greed, anger and ignorance.

What is the purpose of renunciation? Renunciation in the Buddhist sense means to 'leave home' and become a monk or nun. In other words, to enter the Buddhist monastic system. The purpose of leaving home is to allow the believer to leave behind all worldly distractions and concentrate his/her full energies on the practice of the Buddhist path. It is the way to find *Nibbāna* (涅槃) which is the extinction of worldly desires

Renunciation, a journey to enlightenment

and attachments, removing the eight kinds of suffering (生老病死憂悲惱苦; birth, aging, sickness, death, sorrow, distress, affliction, and suffering). *Nibbāna* was originally equivalent to the state of enlightenment attained by the Buddha, meaning the state that can be reached by extinguishing all illusions and destroying all karma, which is the cause of rebirth. In short, renunciation is the itinerant practice to seek the path (八正道 Noble Eightfold Path) to reach *Nibbāna*.

Regarding renunciation, one sutta explains the Buddha's definition of the true nature of renunciation as follows:

"My aim of renunciation was to gain *Nibbāna* where I had no rebirth, no sickness, no old age, no death, no anxiety, no worries, no impurity, and where only the highest degree of peace and happiness existed."

- Majjhima Nikāya 26 ⟨Ariyapariyesanā Sutta⟩

Then what is the ultimate meaning of *Nibbāna* and how should we practice in order to attain it? One sutta (*Saṃyutta Nikāya* 38:1) outlines the brief and clear gist of *Nibbāna* as follows:

"And what is the noble search? Here someone being himself subject to birth, having understood the danger in what is subject to birth, seeks the unborn supreme security from bondage, *Nibbāna*; being himself subject to ageing, having understood the danger in what is subject to ageing he seeks the unageing supreme security from bondage, *Nibbāna*; being himself subject to sickness, having understood the danger in what is subject to sickness, he seeks the unailing supreme security from bondage, *Nibbāna*; being himself subject to death, having understood the danger in what is subject to death, he seeks the deathless supreme security form bondage, *Nibbāna*; being himself subject to sorrow, having understood the danger in what is subject to sorrow, he seeks the sorrowless supreme security from bondage, *Nibbāna*; being himself subject to defilement, having understood the danger in what is subject to defilement, he seeks the undefiled supreme security from bondage, *Nibbāna*. This is the noble search.

- Saṃyutta Nikāya 38:1

Renouncing secular life to become a monk is usually divided into two aspects: body (身出家) and mind (心出家). Furthermore, we can divide this into four subcategories: 1. 'Renouncing secular life to become a monk' both in terms of body and mind (身心具出家) 2. Becoming a monk in terms of body, but mind is still in secular life (身出家心不出家) 3. Becoming a monk in terms of mind, but body is still in secular life (身在家心出家) 4. Becoming a monk, but both body and mind still in secular life (身心具不出家). Among these, both 1. Renouncing secular life to become a monk both in terms of body and mind, and 3. Becoming a monk in terms of mind, but body is still in secular life are a true 'renunciation of secular life to become a monk'.

Regarding renunciation, one sutta (*Sutta-Nipāta*) explains the definition in the verse as follows in terms of cause (s) and condition (s):

> 9 (43). [Even some wanderers are not kindly disposed],
> and also (some) householders dwelling in a house.
> Having little concern for the children of others,
> one should wander solitary as a rhinoceros horn.

- Sutta-Nipāta 1:3 *The Rhinoceros-horn* 9 (43)

This verse depicts people who became monks physically

but their mind is still in the secular world. They are like a layperson full of dissatisfaction. When there is no good friend to help them practice, they should go on alone, like the horn of a rhinoceros. The story behind this verse is as follows:

When the king of Vārāṇasī, who felt disgusted in his royal palace life, gave up his throne and became a monk, many retainers followed him in his renunciation. However, the king later saw that his retainers were dissatisfied with the reality of not being able to satisfy their desires. They had only renounced physically but not in the mind. So the king went into the forest alone, and at the end of his practice, he gained insight into the 'Law of Dependent Arising' (緣起法) and attained enlightenment.

The Law of Dependent Arising is also called the law of causality or law of dependent origination. Along with the 'Four Noble Truths', it is the cardinal principle of Buddhism which Buddha realized after six years of hard practice and meditation. The basic tenet of this doctrine is, along with the theory of emptiness and the non-substantiality of all things, that all phenomena in the universe are constantly changing and have no inherent self-identity. It is a totally different way of expressing truth and ultimate reality. In other words, any existence in the whole universe is a causally conditioned existence, depending on and complementing each other.

The Buddha says,

> "Whosoever perceives dependent arising also perceives suffering, its arising, its ceasing and the path [leading to its ceasing]."

Another sutta (*Sutta-Nipāta*) explains as follows:

> 20 (424). Having seen danger in sensual pleasures, having seen renunciation as safety, I shall go forth in order to strive. In that my mind delights.

- Sutta-Nipāta 3:1 ˌGoing-forthˌ 20 (424)

I. What is a *Bhikkhunī*(Buddhist nun)?

2.
On Becoming
a Monk and Practice

"*Bhikkhus*, begging for alms is the lowest form of livelihood. In this world, to call someone an 'alms-gatherer' is an insult.' And yet, *Bhikkhus*, people intent on doing good choose this life for valid reasons. It is not because they have been driven to it by kings or thieves; it is not due to debt, or fear or even to earn a livelihood. They do so with the thought: 'I am immersed in [the suffering of] birth, aging, and death; [I live] in sorrow, lamentation, pain, displeasure and despair. I am immersed in suffering, oppressed by suffering. Perhaps an end to this suffering can be found?'

"*Bhikkhus*, it is for this reason that people renounce the secular world. And yet there are some who do this who are still covetous, inflamed with lust for sensual pleasures, with a mind full of ill will, with intentions corrupted by hate, lacking clear understanding, unfocused and undisciplined in the sensory faculties. Just like a branch from a funeral pyre that is burning at both ends and smeared with excrement in the middle, it cannot be used as timber, neither in the village nor in the forest. That is how I speak about such people. They have left behind the enjoyments of a householder, and yet they are not true ascetics."

"*Bhikkhus*, there are three kinds of unwholesome thoughts: sensual thoughts, thoughts of ill will and thoughts of doing harm. And where, *Bhikkhus*, do these three unwholesome thoughts cease to exist? They do not exist in one who has attained the four perfections of mindfulness, or in one who has mastered single-minded concentration. This is reason enough, *Bhikkhus*, to develop single-minded concentration. When this is developed and mastered, *Bhikkhus*, it yields great fruit and benefit."

- *Saṃyutta Nikāya* 22:80

Once upon a time the Buddha was in the garden of Nigrodha Temple in Kapilavatthu, the city where the Sakya family lived and Buddha's original home. When the Buddha arrived there with his followers, many Sakya family members came to see him and brought many gifts. An argument broke out as visitors handed out gifts to the *Bhikkhus*. When the Buddha saw this, he rebuked the *Bhikkhus* and dispersed them.

Later, however, he seems to have had a change of heart. The next morning, after he had begged for alms and eaten what he received, he meditated. That is when this thought occurred to him: "Among the public may be a new novice *Bhikkhu* who has just renounced the secular world, and there are some *Bhikkhus* who have just joined me. If young monks cannot see the Buddha, as sometimes a young calf cannot see its mother,

Practice begins with a humble mind .

there may be bad consequences. And if young seeds are not watered, there are also bad consequences." So the Buddha himself had helped the *Bhikkhus* through his teachings.

After he finished meditating, he called the *Bhikkhus* together. After having been scolded, they were timid and sat quietly. The Buddha soon began to speak to them, the content of which is in the above scripture (*Saṃyutta Nikāya* 22:80). When we read this scripture, sometimes we feel good, sometimes we feel bad. This was due to Buddha's remorse about the incident the day before in which several *Bhikkhus* let themselves be controlled by their physical senses.

The above sutta (*Saṃyutta Nikāya* 22:80) is a basic teaching for Buddhists and gives us a glimpse into the Buddha's heart to help us understand what the purpose of Buddhist practice is. It was the Buddha's answer to the fundamental question of why he came into this world.

Buddha came to teach: the truth of suffering, the truth of the path to the arising of suffering, the truth of the cessation of suffering, and the truth of the path to the cessation of suffering. These are called the 'Four Noble Truths' (四聖諦 catari ariya saccani) and are the main content of the Buddha's first sermon at Vārāṇasī. This sermon is also called 'the first turning of the wheel of *Dhamma*' (初傳法輪). Sakyamuni's first sermon was delivered at Deer Park to his five original disciples. Here he also taught that the way to achieve the cessation of suffering was by practicing the Noble Eightfold Path.

This sutta (*Saṃyutta Nikāya* 56:11) contains the content of his first sermon and provides details about the sermon. It says:

> "Now this, *Bhikkhus*, is the noble truth of suffering: birth is suffering, aging is suffering, illness is suffering, death is suffering, union with what is displeasing is suffering;

Ⅰ. **What is a *Bhikkhunī*(Buddhist nun)?**

separation from what is pleasing is suffering; not to get what one wants is suffering; in brief, the five aggregates subject to clinging are suffering."

"Now this, *Bhikkhus*, is the noble truth of the origin of suffering: it is this craving which leads to being reborn, accompanied by delight and lust, seeking delight here and there; that is, craving for sensual pleasures, craving for existence, craving for extermination."

"Now this, *Bhikkhus*, is the noble truth of the cessation of suffering: it is the remainderless fading away and cessation of that same craving, the giving up and relinquishing of it, freedom from it, non-reliance on it."

"Now this, *Bhikkhus*, is the noble truth of the way leading to the cessation of suffering: it is the Noble Eightfold Path, which includes: right view, right intention, right speech, right action, right livelihood, right effort, right mindfulness and right concentration."

- Saṃyutta Nikāya 56:11

These are the Four Noble Truths (suffering, source of suffering, cessation of suffering, and the way to overcome suffering) which are the main content of the Buddha's first sermon. They are the basic tenets of Buddhism that explain the cause of suffering and how to overcome it.

The first Noble Truth is that suffering exists. It is Sakyamuni's realization that existence as we normally perceive it cannot but

Practice is to remove all defilements.

be dissatisfactory. What does the proposition "this is the holy truth of suffering?" tell us? It is a suggestion to face reality. Of course, as in the case of the eight forms of suffering, it is necessary to gain insight into the nature of reality that life itself is full of suffering. Only when we have that will it lead to real insight that will enable us to escape suffering.

The second Noble Truth is the cause of suffering. What is the proposition that "this is the holy truth of the source of suffering?" This requires insight into the undeniable reality

Practice, working meditation with good *Dhamma* friends

of life and then asking what is the root cause of suffering. Often, suffering in any form, whether mental or physical, can be attributed to the inability to get what you want. The greater one's desire, the greater the likelihood that one's suffering will grow, just like a thirsty man searching for water. In Buddhism, the term "craving" is often used to express this.

The third Noble Truth is the cessation of suffering. The principle espoused by Sakyamuni is that all suffering eventually ceases. His proposition that "this is the holy truth of the annihilation of suffering," means that the cause of suffering is thoroughly rooted out only after one begins Buddhist practice and reaches the stage of inner peace and tranquility. It is the overcoming of burning desire and attachment. This is easy to say, but, like the last teaching of the Buddha, it requires devoted and unceasing effort in practice.

The fourth Noble Truth is the path that leads to the end of suffering. The proposition that "this is the holy truth of the way to the annihilation of suffering," is the way that leads to victory over suffering.

To attain this, it is very important to control one's sensory organs completely, and that way is the "Noble Eightfold Path," which was taught by Sakyamuni in his first sermon, and which remains the cornerstone of Buddhist practice. It is no exaggeration to say that the Noble Eightfold Path is the basis of all that Buddha taught for 45 years. Thus, it is the most important teaching and doctrine of Buddhism.

The definition of the Noble Eightfold Path is as follows:

1) What is "right view?" It is the understanding of suffering, the understanding of the source of suffering, the understanding of the annihilation of suffering, and the understanding of the path leading to the annihilation of suffering. It is also the correct understanding of the Four Noble Truths. Therefore, having "right view" means having "right wisdom" which is complete insight into the teachings of "dependent co-arising" and the Four Noble Truths. Dependent co-arising is a valid universal truth of cosmic life, and it implies that the impermanence and transiency of all phenomena in the universe is an unquestionable fact. Buddha attained enlightenment and with it an understanding of the principle of cause and

Practice requires extreme devotion to....

effect between man and the world. The phenomena of birth and death (or appearance and disappearance) are simply results of the unceasing interaction of causes and conditions, also called a "causal relationship." And all existences and phenomena are the result of inter-relatedness or mutual dependency.

2) What is "right thought?" It is the abandonment of all desire, all anger, and all thoughts of violence. In this, our normal everyday thinking is very important. We must neither be distracted nor tempted by the five desires and pleasures that arise from our five senses, and

we must instead cultivate the heart of compassion and benevolence.

3) What is "right speech?" Right speech is the product of right view and right thinking. It refers to "not lying, not making mischief, not swearing, and not saying pointless or foolish things." Words spoken at the right time and place are dignified and worthy. If not, it is better to remain silent.

4) What is "right action?" It means to not kill, not steal, and not indulge in sexual activity for sensual pleasure. The act necessarily follows the intent of the three poisonous actions, the three terrible poisons-greed, anger and folly. Right action means intentional abandonment of the three poisons. Therefore we must strive endlessly to overcome any thoughts of killing, stealing and pursuing gratuitous sexual acts.

5) What is "right livelihood?" It means to abandon any livlihood that causes harm to others. Buddhism teaches the concept of the "five sales" that people should not pursue: the sale of weapons, the sale of humans or animals, the sale of meat, the sale of alcohol and the sale of poison. Swindling, fortunetelling and usury are also wrong.

6) What is "right effort?" It is to apply proper zeal and energy to make continual progress toward *Nibbāna*. Specifically it refers to one's efforts to: suppress the three afflictions (ignorance, anger, greed), discard the afflictions you have, develop good karma through thought, word and deed and then maintain this good *kamma*. Proper devotion to the path demands accruing good *kamma* and ceaselessly rejecting and suppressing evil.

7) What is "right mindfulness?" It is to observe beings as they are and to dwell in constant full awareness and mindfulness of the world without greed or discouragement. The lesson is not to be obsessed with what is not and to be aware of the fact that there is neither reality nor consistency in the body, the feelings, the mind, and the *Dhamma* (all existences). We must contemplate all *Dhamma*s as being without any inherent self or reality.

8) What is "right concentration?" It is meditative concentration that Buddhists call *"samādhi"* It is meditative concentration in a good and healthy state of mind. It is an intense meditative state that transforms the "five hindrances" of the mind into the "five elements of *samādhi*."

The five hindrances are the five mental impediments that

hinder meditation:

1) greed or desire,

2) anger or malice,

3) sloth, torpor or depression,

4) agitation, restlessness or remorse,

5) doubt or perplexity.

In contrast to these five hindrances, the five elements of *samādhi* are:

1) initial course contemplation,

2) subsequent minute discursive contemplation (These first two are mental functions that involve a keen examination of objects – both coarse and minute contemplation.)

3) joy and happiness,

4) pleasure, which is (a kind of) bliss of liberation,

5) single-pointed focus of the mind or fixing one's mind on a single object or condition. This requires stilling the mind to observe an object. The stilling of the mind is *samatha*, and the observation of an object is *vipassanā*. These are two basic forms of Buddhist meditation taught in the Indian tradition: *samatha* and *vipassanā*. The former is usually translated into English as "stabilizing meditation" or "calm abiding." This refers to meditative

practices aimed at the stilling of thought and the development of concentration.

I. What is a *Bhikkhunī*(Buddhist nun)?

3.
A *Bhikkhunī* and a *Bhikkhu*

"Faith is the seed, austerity the rain,
wisdom my yoke and plough;
Shame is the pole, mind the yoke-tie,
Mindfulness my plough share and goad.

Guarded in body, guarded in speech,
Controlled in my appetite for food,
I use truth as my weeding-hook,
And gentleness as my unyoking.

Energy is my beast of burden,
Carrying me to security from bondage.
It goes ahead without stopping
To where, having gone, one does not sorrow."

- Saṃyutta Nikāya 7:11

Mendicancy is the practice of non-possession.

Through the monastic meal,
we learn gratitude for all things.

Ⅰ. What is a *Bhikkhunī*(Buddhist nun)?

One day the Buddha approached a house to beg for alms. As it was the time for sowing, the owner of the house, a *brāhmin*, was carrying several plows on his yoke. When he saw the Buddha, the *brāhmin* seemed to criticize him saying as follows:

"*Dear Bhikkhu*, I plow my fields, sow the seeds, and eat my own food. You should also do the same if you want to eat."

Now on that occasion the *brāhmin* Kasi Bhāradvāja's food distribution was taking place. Then the Blessed One approached the place of the food distribution and stood to one side. The *brāhmin* Kasi Bhāradvāja saw the Blessed One standing for alms and said to him:

"Recluse, I plough and sow, and when I have ploughed and sown I eat. You too, ascetic, ought to plough and sow; then, when you have ploughed and sown, you will eat."
"I too, *brāhmin*, plough and sow, and when I have ploughed and sown I eat."
"But we do not see Master Gotama's yoke or plough or plough share or goad or oxen; yet Master Gotama says, 'I too, *brāhmin*, plough and sow, and when I have ploughed and sown I eat.'"

Then the *brāhmin* Kasi Bhāradvāja addressed the Blessed One in verse:

"You claim to be a man who works the plough,
But I do not see your ploughing.
If you're a ploughman, answer me:
How should we understand your ploughing?"

Saṃyutta Nikāya 7:11

When Buddhism arrived in China and Chan (Zen) Buddhism appeared, monks established a rule saying, "If you do not work one day, you do not eat one day." This refers to "working meditation" which is the physical work that is a part of everyday life in a Chan monastery. The *brāhmin's* remark implied the same, but the Buddha responded without hesitation:

> "Dear *Brāhmin*, I also farm paddies and grow food by sowing seeds."

The *brāhmin* heard this, looked at the Buddha dumbfounded for a while and said, "We have not seen your yoke, plow, cattle drover, rod or bull. How can you say you grow your own food?"

And he asked the Buddha again with the following verse:

> "You say you are a field man.
> I didn't see you go to the field.
> If you are one who goes to the field, tell me,
> How can you see your way through the fields?"

The Buddha answered him with the following verse:

> "Faith is the seed, and asceticism is the rain.
> Wisdom is my yoke and my plow.
> The heart is the rope of the yoke, the shame is the stick,
> Mindfulness is moisturizing and driving the bull.

Take control of your body,
Watch your words, eat your food properly,
Truth is my herbicide, and gentleness removes the yoke of afflictions.
Earnest practice and rigorous self-discipline is my burden
They lead me from bondage to peace.

There is no sadness if one has a restless mind and practices.
When the plowing is over, the fruit of immortality is reaped.
I am free from all suffering."

Although the Buddha chose the life of a mendicant and was looking for food from house to house, the *brāhmin* could see his faith and confidence as a practitioner who has nothing to be ashamed of. This is a scene that illustrates the beauty and honor of the Buddha.

There is a saying that "Empty carts are the noisiest 'and another says', As rice ripens, its head bends lower and becomes humble." When you float rice seeds in salt water, the hollow ones float, and the ones that are full sink. The dignity of the Buddha's begging for alms might be a sign of a healthy and honorable character. Because Buddhism was later transmitted to China, Korea and Japan, some monks who were forced to dress in gold clothes knew how worthless it was.

According to the Buddha, the seed he sows is faith, and the rain that sprouts the seeds is asceticism. His yoke and plow are wisdom. The ropes that control the yoke are the mind, and the rod that drives the bull is mindfulness. Control of one's body and speech and sincerity are the herbicides that mitigate bad *kamma*. This refers to the precept of moral restraint. Observing the precepts indirectly restrains or limits unwholesome acts, and directly promotes wholesome acts.

The ox is like one's zealous practice that leads one to a peaceful and painless place where one can finally escape suffering and find immortality. The idea is that clearing the land, farming and harvesting can be compared to eliminating the three poisons of "greed, anger and folly" by following the precepts.

The original meanings of the Pali words for *Bhikkhu* and nun *Bhikkhunī* were "one who begs for food." However, today those interpretations are no longer relevant; they only mean monk and nun/female monk. The term was originally used in India to refer to the fourth stage of brahmanistic life, wherein the householder would renounce the world, become a beggar and seek enlightenment.

In Buddhism, it came to refer to Buddhist monks and nuns, and to carry an alms bowl was synonymous with religious mendicancy. In the early stages of the development of ancient India's Buddhist *sangha*, itinerant monks would eat one meal a day by carrying their alms bowls past the homes of lay people and accepting whatever food was offered. However, with the establishment of permanent monastic settlements, monasteries were allowed to accept food from the laity, store it, and provide regular communal meals for the monks in residence.

Fundamentally, begging for alms in a village was an act of showing humility and allowing others to show compassion to lead sentient beings to enlightenment. It is also based on the Buddhist philosophy of non-possession. So a fully ordained monk should not forget even for a moment that to carry an alms bowl is one of the twelve disciplines of restraint concerning food, clothing and shelter to practice two of the basic teachings of the Buddha which were non-attachment to the secular world and non-possession.

In today's society, it would be difficult to go house to house begging for food as the basis of one's religious life and practice. However, today's society does not require this, and it can not be denied that monks and nuns already made this practice unnecessary a long time ago. It was only a tradition and practice of early Buddhism, but we should remember to carry on the spirit of non-attachment and non-possession. In Buddhism, the true purpose of teaching non-possession and non-attachment is to avoid accumulating unnecessary things and excessive desire.

Begging for alms is not merely asking for food; it is a skillful means to attain liberation and enlightenment that transcends discrimination, greed, attachment and defilement. It is a relationship between ordained Buddhists and the Buddhist laity which gives economic support to the Buddhist order and to *Bhikkhus* and *Bhikkhunīs*. It also satisfies the spiritual desires of the laity by providing them Buddhist teachings. Through this relationship we can better understand the true meaning of the tradition and philosophy of begging for alms. This reveals the true character and true identity of *Bhikkhus* and *Bhikkhunīs*.

In these days, it must be a harsh thing that begging with a bowl should be the basis of a renuncian monk's life and practice. However, today's society does not require such a life, and it can not be denied that the practitioner himself has already made the practice of begging with a bowl unnecessary a long time ago. It was just the tradition and practice of early Buddhism, but it should be reminded that we should succeed the spirit of non-attachment and non-possession. The true meaning of non-possession and non-attachment is to avoid unnecessary possession, and excessive desire.

That is why we are deeply moved by the lesson of *Vimalakīrti-nirdeśa-sūtra* (維摩經) in the form of a confession as follows:

"Oh blessed Buddha, I remember when I was begging in a poor village. Then the layman bodhisatta Vimalakīrti approached me and said:

'Honorable Mahā-Kassapa. Even if you have compassion, it is not enough to leave the rich and begging from the poor. We must stay in equality and act in turn. When you enter the village, you have to go into the idea that it is an empty village where people do not live. When you look at the image, you see it with the blind, the sound you hear is like an echo, the smell feels like the wind, the taste is not discerned, You have to be aware of it, and everything must be like a fantasy.

A beggar's meal of rice will not be said to have given to all rebirths, to be eaten to all Buddha and saint, and then to be eaten in vain in other people' s donation. Those who can eat like this can enter liberation without abandoning their defilements, and they can be taught right without ceasing their attachment. There are not many abundances of people who see. When he left the damage or gain, he said that he went right in the way of enlightenment and did not rely on the way to seek his own enlightenment.'

Oh, Buddha, I heard this from the layman bodhisatta Vimalakīrti, and I did not encourage others to prctice of a voice-hearer (聲聞), disciple, or solitary realizer (獨覺)."

- *Vimalakīrti-nirdeśa-sūtra* (維摩經 弟子品)

All the scriptures quoted here are passages that help us understand the attitude and virtue of begging for alms. Begging for alms is not merely a asking for food, but a skillful means to attain liberation and enlightenment beyond discrimination, greed, attachment and defilement. It is a kind of relationship between the ordained Buddhists and lay Buddhists (lay male disciple and adult female lay disciple) as economic support for the Buddhist order and the renunciant monk (*Bhikkhu* and *Bhikkhunī*) who satisfy the spiritual desire of layperson by providing Buddhist teaching. Through this relationship, we can understand the true meaning of begging for alms's tradition and philosophy. This is the real entity of *Bhikkhu* and *Bhikkhunī* .

I. What is a *Bhikkhunī*(Buddhist nun)?

A Great Vow: "I vow to eliminate all afflictions."

4.
The First *Bhikkhunīs* and Their Stories

"Lord, it were well that women should obtain the going forth from home into homelessness in this *Dhamma* and discipline proclaimed by the Truth-finder."

"Be careful, Gotami, of the going forth of women from home into homelessness in this *Dhamma* and discipline proclaimed by the Truth-finder." And a second time.... And a third time did the Gotamid, Pajāpatī the Great speak thus to the Lord: "Lord, it were well...."

"Be careful, Gotami, of the going forth of women from home into homelessness in this *Dhamma* and discipline proclaimed by the Truth-finder."

Then the Gotamid, Pajāpatī the Great, thinking: "The Lord does not allow women to go forth from home into homelessness in the *Dhamma* and discipline proclaimed by the Truth-finder," afflicted, grieved, with a tearful face and crying, having greeted the Lord, departed keeping her right side towards him.

Then the Lord having stayed at Kapilavatthu for as long as he found suiting, set out on tour for Vesālī. The Lord stayed there in Vesālī in the Great Grove in the Gabled Hall. Then the Gotamid, Pajāpatī the Great, Having had her hair cut off, having donned saffron robes, set out for Vesālī with several Sakyan women, and in due course approached Vesālī, the Great Grove, the Gabled Hall. Then the Gotamid, Pajāpatī the Great, her feet swollen, her limbs covered with dust, with tearful face, and crying, stood outside the porch of the gateway.

The venerable Ānanda saw the Gotamid, Pajāpatī the Great, standing outside the porch of the gateway, her feet swollen, her limbs covered with dust, with tearful face and crying; seeing her, he spoke thus to the Gotamid, Pajāpatī the Great:

"Why are you, Gotami, standing... and crying?"

"It is because, honoured Ānanda, the Lord does not allow the going forth of women from home into homelessness in the *Dhamma* and discipline proclaimed by the Truth-finder."

"Well now, Gotami, stay here a moment, until I have asked the Lord for the going forth of women from home into homelessness in the *Dhamma* and discipline proclaimed by the Truth-finder."

Then the venerable Ānanda approached the Lord; having approached, having greeted the Lord, he sat down at a respectful distance. As he was sitting down at a respectful distance, the venerable Ānanda spoke thus to the Lord:

"Lord, this Gotamid, Pajāpatī the Great, is standing outside the porch of the gateway, her feet swollen, her limbs covered with dust, with tearful face and crying, and saying that the Lord does not allow the going forth of women from home into homelessness in the *Dhamma* and discipline proclaimed by the Truth-finder. It were well, Lord, if women might obtain the going forth from home... by the Truth-finder."

"Be careful, Ānanda, of the going forth of women from home... by the Truth-finder." And a second time... And a third time the venerable Ānanda spoke thus to the Lord: "It were well, Lord, if women might obtain the going forth... proclaimed by the Truth-finder."

"Be careful, Ānanda, of the going forth of women from home into homelessness in the *Dhamma* and discipline proclaimed by the Truth-finder." Then the venerable Ānanda, thinking:

"The Lord does not allow the going forth of women from home into homelessness in the *Dhamma* and discipline proclaimed by the Truth-finder. Suppose now that I, by some other method, should ask the Lord for the going forth of women from home into homelessness in the *Dhamma* and discipline proclaimed by the Truth-finder." Then the venerable Ānanda spoke thus to the Lord:

"Now, Lord, are women, having gone forth from home into homelessness in the *Dhamma* and discipline proclaimed by the Truth-finder, able to realise the fruit of stream-attainment or the fruit of once-returning or the fruit of non-returning or perfection?"

"Women, Ānanda, having gone forth... are able to realise... perfection."

"If, Lord, women, having gone forth... are able to realise... perfection—and, Lord, the Gotamid, Pajāpatī the Great, was of great service: she was the Lord's aunt, foster-mother, nurse, giver of milk, for when the Lord's mother passed away she suckled him—it were well, Lord, that women should obtain the going forth from home into homelessness in the *Dhamma* and discipline proclaimed by the Truth-finder."

"If, Ānanda, the Gotamid, Pajāpatī the Great, accepts eight important rules, that may be ordination for her:

- Culllavagga X: I -3

I. **What is a** *Bhikkhunī* **(Buddhist nun)?**

Now I want to examine the circumstances surrounding the appearance of the first *Bhikkhunī* (female Buddhist monk). The first male Buddhist monks were five practitioners who heard Buddha's first sermon at Deer Park in Vārāṇasī, and the first female monks were the Buddha's aunt, Mahāpajāpatī-Gotamī, and 500 women of the Sakya clan. The appearance of the first ordained female monk (Pāli. *Bhikkhunī*) came much later than that of the first ordained male monk (Pāli. *Bhikkhu*).

I will offer a brief explanation of the establishment of the early Buddhist order. The appearance of the first *Bhikkhu* came the year after the Buddha attained complete enlightenment after six years of devoted meditation practice; he was 35. One year later he met his first five disciples and preached to them his first sermon. Their names were Koṇḍañña, Vappa, Bhaddiya, Mahānāma and Assaji. They eventually attained the status of *Arahant*, sentient beings who have overcome all afflictions and no longer need further practice. That same year, four friends (Vimala, Subāhu, Puṇṇaji and Gavampati), a man named Yaśa, and 50 of their friends also became students of the Buddha. This can be considered the first actual Buddhist order.

Mahāvana vihāra (monastery) in Vesali, central India. This is where the Buddha's aunt, Mahāpajāpatī Gotamī, the first *Bhikkhunī*, was permitted by the Buddha to join the Buddhist order.

Hearing that Yaśa had renounced secular life to become a monk, his parents came to Deer Park to take him home. However, the Buddha preached to them, and they became the first lay Buddhists to take refuge in the "Three Treasures of Buddhism": the Buddha, the *Dhamma* (Buddha's teachings) and the *Saṅgha* (Buddhist community). After 60 disciples had attained the status of Arahat, the Buddha began full-scale propagation of the *Dhamma* and ordered them to go forth and teach.

Ⅰ. What is a *Bhikkhunī*(Buddhist nun)?

Sixty disciples then went out to 60 places to propagate Buddhism as the Buddha had instructed. He also sought out the original five *Bhikkhus* to do the same and visited Uruvelā Senānigama village in Buddhagaya where he had attained enlightenment and became the Buddha. Here he taught the three Kassapa brothers (Uruvela-Kassapa, Nadi-Kassapa and Gaya-Kassapa) and 1,000 of their apostles. Among them, 250 became the Buddha's disciples, including Sāriputta who later became the Buddha's head disciple. This is the background of the 1,250 *Bhikkhus* spoken of in the *Diamond Sutta*, which is the population of the *Saṅgha* mentioned.

In that same year, Maha-Kassapa became the Buddha's disciple and King Bimbisara presented to the Buddha the first Buddhist temple, Veluvana-vihāra of Rājagaha.

When the Buddha was 38, three years after his enlightenment, Elder Sudatta donated to the Buddha the Jetavana Temple of Sāvatthī in Kosala, and it became a key center for teaching the *Dhamma*. The Buddha dwelt there longer than any other place in his life. In the same year, King Pasenadi of the Kosala Kingdom converted to Buddhism. When the Buddha was 40, five years after his enlightenment, the following members of the Sakya clan joined his monastic community:his half-brother Nanda (the son of Buddha' s aunt Mahāpajāpatī-Gotamī), his only son Rāhula, his cousins Ānanda and Anuruddha, and the barber Upāli. They later became outstanding disciples and played key roles in establishing the early Buddhist order.

At that time the early Buddhist order was plagued by many evils including robbery, murder, lying, etc. Therefore, five to six years after the Buddha's enlightenment, the Buddhist order began to establish precepts to prevent such activities. With the establishment of a framework for the Buddhist order and its community (*Saṅgha*), the Buddha's 45 years of teaching and the communal practices of early Buddhism provided the foundation for modern Buddhism.

Historically, the *Saṅgha* consisted of two "pillars," male and female monks (*Bhikkhus* and *Bhikkhunis*). However, the *Bhikkhuni* order was established much later than the *Bhikkhu* order. But eventually, 500 Sakya women including the Buddha's aunt, Mahāpajāpatī-Gotamī, were allowed by the Buddha to renounce the secular world and become monks. This was a very important event that helps us understand the establishment of the *Bhikkhuni* order. Now I would like to introduce the first incident related to the founding of the

I. **What is a *Bhikkhunī*(Buddhist nun)?**

Bhikkhuni community by reviewing its historical context.

One day the Buddha visited his hometown of Kapilavatthu. At that time he was 40 years old, five years after he had attained enlightenment. Upon arrival he was immediately informed that his father King Suddhodana was seriously ill and bedridden, so he moved to Nigrodha Monastery on the outskirts of Kapilavatthu. That summer, however, a severe drought continued. The farmers of the Sakya clan and the neighboring Colia clan were arguing over water rights to the Lohini River and who could use how much to water their rice paddies. The two clans were on the verge of going to war.

The Buddha asked the kings of both clans, "Which is more precious, human beings or the river? Only a clan who loves peace and justice can prosper." He then advised them, "Let us live happily, free from hatred, misery, and greed, even among those full of hatred, agony, and greed." The dispute was settled. Actually, both clans were descendants of the same ancestor, King Okkaka.

The two clans sought peace again and praised the majesty and virtue of the Buddha. Each clan then selected 250 young noblemen to serve the Buddha, but the Buddha rejected the offer. Instead he wanted them to join him as voluntary *Dhamma* disciples. They were talented young men living with their parents, and some even had wives.

Not long after the feud over water rights, King Suddhodana died. After his death, the Buddha offered to carry the coffin himself, but relatives persuaded him to carry only an incense burner to the crematorium. He later returned to the forest where he stayed after completing all of the funeral rites.

Later, his aunt Mahāpajāpatī-Gotamī visited him with a nice Buddhist robe she had made herself. However, the Buddha refused to accept the robe and handed it over to the Buddhist order. Mahāpajāpatī-Gotamī was very disappointed at this, and as she cried, she then told him the real reason for her visit. Though she had lived long under the shadow of the late king, she and many of the women who remained alone in the royal palace had begged the Buddha to be allowed to join his community.

In ancient times, in India, China and even Korea, it was expected for a woman to be subservient to three men in her life: her father when young, her husband after marriage, and her son after her husband dies. After the late king passed away, even his two sons (Buddha and Nanda) and grandson were allowed to live in the shadow of the Buddha. She was begging him for compassion for her own situation because now she had no one to rely on. So she was asking live in the shadow of the Buddha.

Buddha refused her request, but Mahāpajāpatī-Gotamī begged again and again three times in tears. In the big forest outside Kapilavatthu where the Buddha resided, all appeals from females to enter the monastic order were rejected by the Buddha. Then the Buddha took 500 new male renunciants from the Sakya and Colia clans to Vesāli. It was later that a remarkable spectacle took place.

One day, the Buddha shaved his head, put on coarse clothes, and went barefoot into the streets. At that time, the former royal lady, Gotamī appeared looking like a begging monk and she was followed by 500 females of the Sakya and Colia clans. They were headed for a large forest temple in the suburbs of Vesāli where Buddha dwelled. The distance from Kapilavatthu to Vesāli was about 450 miles. As they walked barefoot along the road, their feet became swollen and blistered, and their bodies were covered with dust and dirt. They stood at the door of the monastery and wept for permission to join the monastic order.

When Ānanda saw this, he felt sorry for Mahāpajāpatī-Gotamī and asked the Buddha again to allow females into the monastic order and was again rejected. Ānanda was later appointed chief disciple and attended on the Buddha 24 hours a day. The Buddha was then 55 years old and this was 20 years after his enlightenment. Gotamī was was then nearly 75. From Gotamī's point of view, her nephew Ānanda was now in a good position to make this request again to the Buddha. Ānanda asked the Buddha again but the Buddha again rejected it. Instead, the Buddha tried to persuade Ānanda with logic to abandon the proposal. However, Ānanda then asked the Buddha this question: "If women practice as renunciant monks, do they attain the level of *Sotāpanna* (the first of the four stages in Hīnayāna practice) or *Arahant* (the highest level in Hīnayāna practice)?"

The Buddha answered, and Ānanda then made the following statement: "If women can attain the level of *Arahant*, I hope your Aunt Gotamī will be the first female renunciant monk."

At this earnest request, the Buddha finally relented. However, he established the condition that all female monks must observe eight precepts (比丘尼八敬法 Pāli. *aṭṭha garu-dhammā*):

(1) even if they are 100 years old, a nun must pay respect to a monk, however young, and offer her seat to him;
(2) she must never scold a male monk;
(3) she must never accuse or speak of his misdeeds
(4) she must be ordained by a male monk;
(5) she must confess any sin before an assembly of monks and nuns;
(6) she must have a monk as her preceptor;
(7) she must never attend the same summer retreat with monks;
(8) after the summer retreat, she must report and ask for a responsible male monk confessor.

This led to the establishment of the first Buddhist order of female monks, and was followed by a rapid influx of other female renunciants. This is why the female order later came to honor Ānanda. In addition, some of the elders from among the *brāhmins*, including Mahākāśyapa, did not agree with this decision, and they urged Ānanda to repent for this sin at the first Buddhist council that was held shortly after the death of the Buddha. Regardless, upon receiving the Buddha's permission, Mahāpajāpatī-Gotamī was as happy as a man and a woman when they wear a lot of lotus flowers on their head.

Mahāpajāpatī-Gotamī first asked the Buddha for permission to renounce the secular world five years after his enlightenment when he was 40, right after her husband King Suddhodana died. Finally, when the Buddha was 55, the first female renunciants were allowed to join. This was due to the persistence of the Sakya women, including Gotamī, Ānanda's assistance and the Buddha's permission. This occurred 20 years after Buddha's enlightenment.

I already mentioned the first appearance of the Buddhist laity. At first, the Buddha did not explain any difference between male and female Buddhists as far as the *Dhamma* is concerned. The word '*Dhamma*' comes from the Indic root word dhr, which means 'that which preserves or maintains,' especially that which preserves or maintains human activity. Long before the appearance of the first female monastic order, there were other female lay Buddhists like Visākha Migāramātā, Bandulra Mallika, Khujjuttarā and Velukandakiya. So there was much speculation about the Buddha's hesitation to accept females. There were also questions about why he insisted on their following the additional Eight Precepts (Pāli. *aṭṭha garu-dhammā*). What was the reason for that?

Now I would like to finish this chapter by reviewing the Buddha's thoughts and feelings regarding the doubt and questions raised above. Following is what the Buddha had to say about fully ordained females joining the Buddhist order (*saṅgha*):

> "I cannot accept a woman's renunciation of the secular world for the following reasons: If women receive the full precepts (today Hīnayāna Buddhism has 250 for monks and 348 for nuns), there could be a lapse or interruption in spreading the Buddha-*Dhamma* (Buddha's teachings). As a comparison, if there are few men and many women in a house, the house will likely perish. It is also the same as when a good grain field is destroyed when battered by hail."
>
> - The Vinaya of the Four Categories. (Dhammaguptaka-vinaya)

The verse quoted above was the Buddha's answer to the request of allowing the renunciation of Mahāpajāpatī-Gotamī and 500 women of the Sākiya clan. The reason a woman should not be allowed to enter the monastic order is because it was believed that the age of true Buddha-*Dhamma* might be interrupted. This would mean that the true Buddha-*Dhamma* would end. Several scriptures explain why the Buddha first refused the women's request. Some of the reasons are: 'the theory that the Buddha-*Dhamma* wound end after 500 years'; 'the theory of the five inabilities of women'; 'the theory of

Female renunciation rewrote the history of the Buddhist Order.

females having to be reborn as males.'

In the first theory, it was originally believed that the age of true Buddha-*Dhamma* would last 1,000 years, but if women entered the order, it would only last 500 years. (*The Lotus Sutra* 法華經 and *Sutra on the Source of the Vinaya* 毘尼母經).

The second theory said that a woman cannot achieve the five stages of: *Śakra Devānām-Indra* (king of heaven; Indra), God *Brahmā, Māra* King, Wheel-turning Sage King and Buddha. (*Ekôttarikâgama* 增一阿含經 and *The Lotus Sutra* 法華經).

The third theory says that, because being born a women is

considered one of the five obstacles to enlightenment, some texts teach that women must be reborn as men before they can become buddhas. Thus, every buddha is supposed to vow to change all women into men.

- The Lotus Sutra

Is that true? If women join the monastic order, will the age of true *Dhamma* be reduced? And if a woman cannot become a buddha, is it reasonable that she can only after she is reborn as a man?

Ānanda asked the Buddha, "If a woman enters the monastic order, can she achieve the 'four stages/realizations' of the *sāvaka* path (stream-enterer, once-returner, non-returner and arhat)?" This question is about the four stages of enlightenment required to become an Arhat. To this, the Buddha replied "Yes." Why did he answer 'Yes' even though he had originally refused their request? What was his real intent?

Now we must look at the internal structure of *brāhman* society and the early Buddhist order in India at that time. First, let's look at the situation outside the Buddhist order. According to the social sentiments and customs in India at that time, women were considered mere housewives. The belief was that if a woman became a mendicant monk, it would destroy her family and break down the social infrastructure. And that was a good enough reason to not allow them into the order. The early Buddhist order was still young and frail at that time and would possibly face social outcry or collapse if it too hastily accepted women. The Buddha thought that such an action would go against social traditions and customs.

One scripture, *Mahāvagga* (大品 Great Chapter), tells us that these concerns were not negligible. In the case of Yaśa (one of the Buddha᾽s early disciples) and his friends leaving home together to become monks, the *brāhman*s and their followers criticized the Buddha saying, "The Buddha is destroying families by taking young men away from their wives and making them widows." Therefore, for preservation of the order, it was a very urgent matter for the Buddha's followers to maintain good relations with the general public and the laity. The monastic order could not alienate the general society as long as they depended on people to give them food.

Recall that Mahāpajāpatī-Gotamī and 500 other Sakya women asked to join the Buddha only five years after the birth of the monastic order. From this perspective, it was prudent for the Buddha to wait for the right time.

What was the internal situation of the Buddhist order then? Mahāpajāpatī-Gotamī was the Buddha's aunt, who for 29 years cherished him more than her own sons. In addition, 500 Sakya women were ex-wives of *Bhikkhus*, many of whom were Buddha's disciples in the monastic order. There also was Yasodara, the Buddha's ex-wife. It was enough for brahmans and other non-Buddhists to criticize him for that reason. If the order accepted women, there would likely be other cases of familial relationships within the order. It was a very confusing situation for outsiders to grasp in a society that looked down on women.

After the Buddhist order was first established, for the first 20 years *Bhikkhus* had practiced mendicancy and wore ragged clothes. That was because non-Buddhists rejected the practice of receiving clothes from the laity, especially in the case of nudists lifestyle of Jainism practitioners who had received the respect of the believers. In addition, unlike today, *Bhikkhus* then slept in the forests, in the hills, in vacant houses or in the houses of ordinary people. Women were less suited to this lifestyle and also feared being raped when they were alone. Even after a female monastic order was established, Buddhist nuns were prohibited from staying in the forests and mountains; they could only reside in places where Buddhism was well established.

Such circumstances both inside and outside the order allow us to understand why the Buddha's initial refusal to accept women was not related to their mental or intellectual abilities; it was due to social and institutional problems and the matter of their personal safety. That is why he established the Eight Precepts for Women (八敬戒) when his aunt was admitted to the order, and they still apply today. It is also enough to explain the validity of the background that the Buddha has long hesitated to accept as a woman the member of the Buddhist order. It was the Buddha's thoughtful actions with such circumstances in mind.

Eight Precepts [specifically for nuns] stipulated in the *Vinayapiṭakaare* as follows:

> "A nun who has been ordained (even) for a century must greet respectfully, rise up from her seat, salute with joined palms, do proper homage to a monk ordained but that day. And this rule is to be honoured, respected, revered, venerated, never to be transgressed during her life."
>
> "A nun must not spend the rains in a residence where there in no monk. This rule too is to be honoured... during her life."
>
> "Every half month a nun should desire two things from the

Order of monks: the asking (as to the date) of the Observance day, and the coming for the exhortation. This rule too is to be honoured... during her life."

"After the rains a nun must 'invite' before both Orders in respect of three matters: what was seen, what was heard, what was suspected. This rule too is to be honoured... during her life."

"A nun, offending against an important rule, must undergo *mānatta* (discipline) for half a month before both Orders. This rule too must be honoured... during her life."

"When, as a probationer, she has trained in the six rules for two years, sh should seek ordination from both Orders. This rule too is to be honoured... during her life."

"A monk must not be abused or reviled in any way by a nun. This rule too is to be honoured... during her life."

"From to-day admonition of monks by nuns is forbidden, admonition of nuns by monks is not forbidden. This rule too is to be honoured, respected, revered, venerated, never to be transgressed during her life."

"If, Ānanda, the Gotamid, Pajāpatī the Great, accepts these eight important rules, that may be ordination for her."

- Culllavagga X:4

These Eight Precepts clearly established the relationship between *Bhikkhus* and *Bhikkhunīs* at that time. We can also see the roles of *Bhikkhus* and *Bhikkhunīs*. If you look only at the specific precepts, the Eight Precepts seem to take for granted the difference between *Bhikkhus* and *Bhikkhunīs*. However, it is clear that the doubts and questions raised about women's entrance into the order can be fully explained and answered by the Eight Precepts. The Eight Precepts, as an expediency, made it easier to accept women into the order and should not be construed as institutional Buddhist sexism.

Thus, there are important facts that we should not overlook in the history of the foundation of the female Buddhist order. We can see not only the thoughtfulness of the Buddha's views toward women, but also the autonomous aspiration and enthusiasm of the women who desperately sought to enter the monastic order. In addition, we can look into the universal values and traditional customs of contemporary society and the lifestyles of non-Buddhist groups as well. The events related to the establishment of the first Buddhist female order are the lessons that teach us even today.

The Path to Become a *Bhikkhunī*

1.
The Path to Become a *Bhikkhunī* : Enlightenment and Ordination

"I delight in quenching cravng. Existence is non-eternal, even if you are a deity. How many more [non-eternal phenomena] are empty sensual pleasures that give little enjoyment [and] how many more sensual pleasures give little enjoyment [and] much distress." (450)

"Sensual pleasures, by which fools are bemused, [are] bitter, like a snake's poison. Consigned to hell for a long time, those [fools] are beaten and suffer pain." (451)

"Because of evil actions, they grieve in a nether realm, enduring evil, without faith. Fools [are] unrestrained in thought, word and deed." (452)

"Those fools, unwise, senseless, hindered by the arising of pain, not knowing, do not understand the noble truths being taught." (453)

"Permit me, both of you, to go forth there and teach of the Ten-Powered One. Having little greed, I shall strive for the elimination of birth and death." (457)

"What [have I to do] with existence, with delight for this unsubstantial worst of bodies? For the sake of ending my craving for existence, permit me. I shall go forth." (458)

- *Therīgāthā* 450-458

In this chapter, I want to explain the path to becoming a female monk, *Bhikkhunī*. I would like to begin this chapter by looking at one impressive story about a woman's desire to become a *Bhikkhunī*. The story is about an elder *Bhikkhunī* and is found in the latter part of the scripture *Therī-gāthā* (Verses by Elder Nuns: a Collection of 522 Religious Poems by Elder Nuns of the Buddhist Monastic Order).

There was a beautiful Indian princess, the daughter of the king of Concha and his first queen who lived in Mantabati, a city state in central India. She was erudite and profound and was always thinking about the Buddha's teachings. One day the king informed her that he had promised to have her marry the king of a neighboring country, King Anika Ratta. After all, it was her destiny to become a queen. However, she said she wanted no part of such a marriage. She told her parents she intended to become a Buddhist monk and was very adamant about it. Her mother cried in pain, and her father was greatly shocked.

The king tried to persuade her by telling her about all the wealth, honor, power and happiness she would have as a queen. She still refused and said that if she was forced to marry, she would stop eating and starve herself to death. King Anika Ratta visited her and asked her to dress up in jewels and gold for the wedding. She adamantly refused and stressed how transient such pleasures were. She cut her long hair and threw it at her parents and fiance to prove her firm determination. Her fiance then understood her resolve and asked her parents to allow her to become a monk. Her parents finally relented, and she attained the status of a saint after perfecting her enlightenment. She was the *Bhikkhunī* Sumedha.

In this story, we can see that the Buddha's teachings had already spread far into central India even before Sumedha become a monk. Mantabati was her homeland, a city state located north of the capital of Avanti State, Ujjeni, which was the hometown of the eminent sage Mahākaccāna. This verse also shows that the Four Noble Truths is the core teaching of Buddhism and also shows how widely the Buddha's teachings had spread. Sumedha's determination and her parents' consent confirm the fact that Buddhist nunneries and female monks were already well established at that time.

The history of a Buddhist female order began with the additional Eight Precepts that Buddha gave to Mahāpajāpatī-

Having one's head shaved is the first step to saving sentient beings and enlightenment.

Gotamī. By receiving and obeying them she had received the 'complete set of precepts' (具足戒) - also known as 'full set of precepts' (大戒) - and was a member of the Buddhist monastic order. An ordination ceremony (*upasampadā*) always involves receiving the precepts, which 'enable' one to follow the Buddhist path and enter monastic life. Likewise, in order to become a member of a monastic order, a *Bhikkhunī* must receive and observe a complete set of precepts. Regarding the receiving and observance of these precepts, the *Sutta on the Source of the Vinaya* (毘尼母經) explains as follows:

> ① *Dhamma* ordination by keeping Eight Precepts (師法受具): Mahāpajāpatī-Gotamī's fulfilled her renunciation of the secular world and her ordination by keeping the Eight Precepts
> ② Ordination ceremony by the Four-announcements (白四羯磨): A ritual ceremony connected with the vinaya which

occurs during an ordination ceremony or when dealing with repentances for sins committed.

③ Ordination by substitute or proxy (遣使受具): If one who is to receive the precepts cannot attend the ordination ceremony for whatever reason, an agent or proxy may receive the ordination in his/her place.

④ Ordination by Invitation (善來受具): This refers to someone who is already a 'stream-enterer' (須陀洹) and is considered ordained by virtue of being invited into the order. Simply put, a 'stream enterer' is one who has already attained the first of the four realizations 四果 of the *sāvaka* 聲聞 path.

⑤ Ordination by hearing the *Dhamma* (上受具): This is an ordination that occurs when one becomes an *arahant* (阿羅漢), the highest type or ideal saint in Hīnayāna, by hearing the Buddha's *Dhamma* preaching.

Since the days of early Buddhism, a complete ordination is generally conducted by a four-announcement ceremony (白四羯磨). An announcement is first made to the monastic assembly and afterward a motion is put to a vote three times. *Dhamma* ordination by keeping the Eight Precepts (師法受具) and the other four ceremonies were popular in Tang China, but later, all of the above five methods were abolished.

At this point I will offer a rough review of the process of becoming a *Bhikkhunī*. Firstly, the permission of the *Bhikkhunī* order is necessary. A woman who wants to become a *Bhikkhunī* should make an earnest request, after a proper

Practitioners reading aloud their vows
(the 50th class to receive the precepts in the Jogye Order of Korean Buddhism in 2016, at Jikji-sa Temple)

One full prostration for every three steps,
lowering myself on the way to enlightenment

salutation, while kneeling before the *Bhikkhuni* order. After permission is granted, her head is shaved and she dons the Buddhist robe in a special ceremony. She then recites the 'Three Refuges Verse' three times in front of the order to become a *Bhikkhunī*. This verse is also recited in a ceremony to confer the precepts to both the laity and renunciant practitioners. The 'Three Refuges' refers to: the Buddha 佛, the *Dhamma* (Buddhist teachings) 法, and the *Saṅgha* (community of monks and nuns) 僧. The number '3' figures prominently in Buddhism, and the Three Refuges are also called the 'Three Treasures' or 'Three Reliances.'

After entering the Buddhist order, the first ceremony a *sāmaṇerī* (novice female renunciant) must undergo is the ceremony of the ten precepts (十戒). These are the ten basic Buddhist precepts for both *Bhikkhus* and *Bhikkhunīs*. They are:

1) Do not kill.

2) Do not steal.

3) Do not commit sexual misconduct.

4) Do not lie.

5) Do not use intoxicants.

6) Do not eat at improper times.

7) Do not use excessive adornments or perfumes.

8) Do not sleep on raised beds.

9) Do not take part in singing, dancing, musical or theatrical performances, or watch or listen to same.

10) Do not possess accessories made of gold, silver or jewels.

The first five of these (五戒) are also observed by lay practitioners, and they are called the fundamental precepts or thebasic five precepts. Naturally, sexual intercourse is prohibited to monks but is allowed for married lay practitioners.

This is called 'the ordination ceremony of *sāmaṇerī*'. The ten precepts *sāmaṇerī* should keep is the same as that of a *sāmaṇera* (male novice monk). The *Mahavagga's Vinaya-piṭaka* (律藏 Collected Precepts) records the following conversation:

> "The novice male monks asked the Buddha, "How many precepts do we have to keep?"The Buddha responded, "There are ten precepts that must be observed in practice. So be careful to cultivate these ten precepts."

> - *Mahavagga* Chapter 1, 56

II. The Path to Become a *Bhikkhunī*

*Sāmaṇerī*s (novice nuns) learning the precepts
and the spirit and manner of renunciation

Ordination ceremony for *sikkhamānā*s
on the way to becoming *Bhikkhunī*s

Originally, both *sāmaṇera* and *sāmaṇerī* referred to novice male and female monks under the age of 20, but these days they may be over 20. In order for a *sāmaṇerī* to become fully ordained, she must pass a special 2-year *sikkhamānā* (式叉摩那) course. Six additional practices that a *sikkhamānā* (式叉摩那 ordained practitioner between the ages of 18 and 20) undertakes as part of her two year training between being a *sāmaṇerī* and *Bhikkhunī*. *Sikkhamānā* is an ordained practitioner between the ages of 18 and 20 who accepts the six precepts of abstinence from sex, stealing, killing, lying, consumption of alcohol, and eating at improper times.

The *sikkhamānā* system did not exist when the first females were allowed into the monastic order. So 'Eight Precept [specifically for nuns]' article mentioned above did not apply to the way to the reception of full ordination of Mahāpajāpatī-Gotamī and other five hundred *Sakya* women. 'Eight Precept [specifically for nuns]' stipulates that *sikkhamānā* could attain the full ordination ofter keeping six precept (六法戒) for two years.

Accordingly, at that time the 'full precepts' (具足戒) only applied to the ordination of both male and female monastics.

II. The Path to Become a *Bhikkhunī*

As the Buddhist order grew, the precepts for novices (沙彌戒) was separated from the full precepts. In addition, the ten precepts taken by the *sāmaṇerikā* (沙彌尼戒), *Sikkhamānā* and nuns were subdivided and became the new standard. A *sikkhamānā* must have a teacher who will guide them and their every action. Such a teacher is also referred to as a beneficent master, respected teacher, or one's original teacher. In order to become a *sikkhamānā*, a *Bhikkhunī* must make the following request three times while kneeling on both knees. kneeling on both knees.

> "I am the *sāmaṇerī* (insert novice nun's name) and I study under (insert teacher's name). I cordially request that the *Bhikkhu* order allow me to practice for two years as a *sikkhamānā* while keeping the six precepts."

Here six precepts are six additional practices that *sikkhamānā* (ordained practitioners between the ages of 18 and 20) undertakes as part of her two year training between being a *sāmaṇerī* and *Bhikkhunī*. According to the *Vinayapiṭaka*, six precepts are as follows:

1. not killing,

2. not stealing,

3. not coming into contact with a male with a defiled mind,

4. not lying,

5. not drinking alcohol,

6. not eating when it is inappropriate [past noon].

Six precepts are exactly the same as the ten precepts of novices (*sāmaṇerī*) including five fundamental precept and one additional precept of not eating when it is inappropriate [past noon]. However, the other four precepts are unnecessary during the period of *sikkhamānā*. What is the meaning of this?

This kind of question can be seen in the *precepts collection* (律藏, 根本說一切有部苾芻尼毘奈耶 (Mūlasarvāstivāda) *Bhikkunī-vinaya-vibhaga* 18). This verse tells about the six precepts concerning safety and the sex:

① Do not walk alone.

② Do not cross the river by yourself.

③ Do not touch the body of the man.

④ Do not sleep with the man.

⑤ Do not stand in the match.

⑥ Do not cover the felony of your nun.

It is largely concentrated on women's safety issues and the cultivation of moral discipline.

Many precepts tell that Buddhist nuns were raped when

they were alone on a remote road, in a forest, or even on a ship crossing a river. One clause in the *Eight Precepts for Nuns*, which prohibits nuns from staying in forests or mountains, or that nuns should not be held in places without *Bhikkhu* (male monk), is a source of this kind of concern. The contents of the *Six Precepts*, such as 'Do not touch the body of a man' or 'Do not sleep with a man', were not prohibited during the period of *sikkhamānā*. It is possible to look at the meaning in the light of the fact that autonomous exceptions were possible to some extent.

This gives some insight into the background of having a special two-year course just before becoming a full-time ordered monk (*Bhikkhunī*). It is a period of contemplation whether to continue to live a life of childbirth or not, and it seems to have been a yardstick to judge whether a woman is pregnant or not. In short, the Buddhist order did not allow women to go straight from a novice to be a *Bhikkhunī*, both mentally and professionally.

Now let's look at the process of becoming a *Bhikkhunī*, the final gateway to the life of renunciation. In order to become a *Bhikkhunī*, she must repeat the following request three times with the salutation by sitting on both knees in front of the general public:

> "I apply the ordination of full precepts to *Bhikkhunī* order. Please accept my earnest request to enter the *Bhikkhunī* order."

Generally the process of taking the full precepts is as follows. First of all *sikkhamānā* should have a monk teacher. The teacher must be a male ordained monk, at least 12 year *Dhamma* age (the number of years that have passed since a person was first ordained as a Buddhist monk; the main way of calculating seniority within the monastic order). The eligible applicant for taking the full precepts is *sikkhamānā* who is allowed by the order to keep the six precepts for two years. The *sikkhamānā* who is eligible for taking the full precepts follows the procedure of ordination at the ordination platform, the altar at which the precepts are received by the novice.

At the ordination ceremony, there must be the teacher transmitting precepts along with ten *Bhikkhunīs* including three monks and seven witness who supervise and testimony the ordination. The teacher will test the eligibility of taking full precept and the *sikkhamānā* should answer the teacher's questions. If the *sikkhamānā* passes the eligibility test, she will receive the precepts to keep according to the code of

Vinaya precepts (Pāli. *pātimokkha*). It refers to the body of precepts to be kept by monks and nuns, specifically, a part of the Vinaya that contains the 227 disciplinary rules for monks and 348 nuns that is recited at every *uposatha (confessional) ceremony*. The full precepts in Korea is the 348 disciplinary rules for *Bhikkhunīs*.

However, this is not the end of *Bhikkhunī ordination*. The *Bhikkhu* (male monk) ordination completed with the single ordination ceremony, but the *Bhikkhunī* ordination should have another second ceremony at same day in the *Bhikkhu* ordination platform. This is called 'the double ordination ceremony'.

This another second *Bhikkhu* ordination platform also needs three monks and seven witness monks who supervise and testimony the ordination. This means altogether six monks and fourteen witness monks who supervise and testimony are required in taking the full precepts.

This tradition has been handed down from India to Sri Lanka, the southern Buddhism of Southeast Asia, and northern Buddhism, including Korea and Japan, of Northeast Asia including China.

2.
The History of
the Ordination Ceremony

In order to become a *Bhikkhunī*, a woman must first receive the permission of the *Bhikkhunī* order. Afterward, she must receive and agree to observe the six precepts of a *sikkhamānā*, a two-year training period between becoming a *sāmaṇerī* and becoming a *Bhikkhunī*. Before receiving the 'full precepts', she must receive the 'double ordination ceremony', the first performed by *Bhikkhus* and the second by *Bhikkhunīs*. Here she receives the 'eight *Bhikkhunī* precepts' for nuns (Pāli. *aṭṭha garu-dhammā*). These are the eight precepts given by the Buddha to his foster-mother/aunt when she was admitted to the order. This 'double ordination ceremony' is required by the Jogye Order of Korean Buddhism. It is a tradition practiced by the Theravāda Buddhists in Southeast Asia and by Mahāyāna Buddhists in Northeast Asia.

Gyeom-ik (謙益), an early Baekje monk of the Vinaya school, traveled to India to learn Sanskrit and the Vinaya(precepts).

He returned to Baekje in 526, bringing back the *Five Part Vinaya* (五分律) and a number of other Vinaya and AbhiDhamma texts. He translated these into literary Chinese, providing an important early impetus for the establishment of Vinaya studies in Korea. Let's take a look at the Japanese text *Gangōji Garan Engi* (元興寺伽藍縁起). Korean records about the *Bhikkhunī* double ordination system are scarce, however, related information does exist in Japan. It also sheds light on the situation of Baekje Buddhism at that time. It states:

> "The ordination ceremony first requires ten *Bhikkhunī* teachers from a *Bhikkhunī* temple to perform the first ordination, and then afterward, ten *Bhikkhu* teachers from a *Bhikkhu* temple administer the full precepts. So altogether the ceremony requires 20 monks. However, because there are only *Bhikkhunīs* in this country (Japan), and there are no *Bhikkhu* temples or *Bhikkhu* masters, *Bhikkhunīs* will be required to set up *Bhikkhu* temples and invite *Bhikkhus* and *Bhikkhunīs* from the Baekje Kingdom."

That is what Baekje envoys told Japanese King Yungming

The first *Sāmaṇerī*s (novice nuns) receiving the precepts on the single precept platform of the Jogye Order of Korean Buddhism (1981, Tongdo-sa Temple)

The first double ordination to receive full precepts on the single platform in the Jogye Order of Korean Buddhism (1982, Beomeo-sa Temple)

The first *sikkhamānā* single ordination platform in the Jogye Order of Korean Buddhism (1995, Beomeo-sa Temple)

Ⅱ. **The Path to Become a *Bhikkhunī***

(用明) in the 2nd year of his reign (587). Accordingly, Japan's 'First Lord' (蘇我馬子) invited a Baekje monk to Japan and asked about the system of precepts in Baekje. Afterward, three Japanese female renunciants (善信·禪藏·惠善) were invited to Baekje in 588 and stayed for three years to study the precepts and become *Bhikkhunīs*. In 590, they returned to Japan. This Japanese record proves the double ordination system existed in Baekje at that time.

After traveling to Tang China to study, the early Silla monk Jajang (慈藏) returned to Silla in 643 and founded a Vinaya (precepts) school. He was a scholar of considerable knowledge about precepts and is credited for being a major force in setting up the Korean *saṅgha* and having Buddhism recognized as Silla's national religion. Jajang also introduced into Silla Daoxuan's (道宣 596–667) Nanshan School (南山宗), one of three major Chinese Vinaya schools. Three years later Jajang returned to Silla where he founded Tongdo-sa Temple and had the Diamond Altar built, the altar where *Bhikkhus* and *Bhikkhunīs* receive the precepts. It is because of Jajang that the Jogye Order of Korean Buddhism inherited the precepts lineage of the Nanshan School.

Goryeo Buddhism also relied on the *Vinaya of the Four Categories* (四分律) which originated with the Nanshan School. It is not easy to find records from the Joseon era about the ordination system because of Joseon's policy of promoting Confucianism and oppressing Buddhism, and that is apparently when the double ordination system for *Bhikkhunīs* disappeared.

It is not easy to find any concrete records of the order system in Joseon Buddhism because of the government's promoting Confucianism and rejecting Buddhism policy. Even though there was some trend of promoting Buddhism in the palace, unlike the Confucian scholars, it is impossible to confirm how the maintenance of order and the platform facilities for ordination survived in the Joseon Buddhism.

If we take a look at the ordination facilities and ordination method in the Buddhist order after the flowering period of the late 19th century, the Japanese colonial period, and the modern period, it seems that the *Bhikkhunī* double ordination system had been cut off (discontinued) by the government re pressive policy of Buddhism and Buddhist monks) during the Joseon Dynasty.

3.
Restoration of and Problems with the *Bhikkhunī* Ordination Tradition

The double ordination system for *Bhikkhunīs* has only been restored relatively recently since vanishing in the Joseon dynasty. Its restoration was made possible by preceptor Ven. Jaun Seongwoo (慈雲盛祐, 1911~1992), well known for his knowledge of the precepts. He made a list of precepts based on *Vinaya of the Four Categories* (四分律). This text explains the origins and causes by which the *Code of Vinaya Precepts* (Pāli. *pātimokkha*) enumerates the offenses covered by the precepts for both *Bhikkhus* and *Bhikkhunīs* — especially classifying them as either light or serious. Ven. Jaun Seongwoo proposed restoring the *Bhikkhunī* double ordination system at the start of 1982, and the Jogye Order agreed in June 1982.

As mentioned earlier, the *Bhikkhunī* double ordination system is based on the *Vinaya of the Four Categories* (四分律) which originated with China's Nanshan School. However, some people have misunderstood the double ordination system as meaning *Bhikkhunīs* are subordinate to *Bhikkhus*, contrary to the Buddha's original intention. That is why some people oppose the double ordination system, especially in this time of the gender equality debate.

According to the *Collected Precepts* (律藏), the real intention of the Buddha regarding the double ordination system is as follows:

> "After the first *Bhikkhunī* order was established, many women sought to renounce secular life and become monks. At that time in early Buddhism, there was only a single ordination ceremony for both males and females to receive the full precepts, and there were no questions about a *Bhikkhunī's* physical or mental capacity. As a result, any woman could apply, regardless of health or past dubious behavior. At that time there was a so-called '24 obstacles rule' which applied only to *Bhikkhus* which could prevent them from becoming a monk based on physical or mental defects."

> Knowing this, the Buddha ordered that the '24 obstacles rule' should also apply to *Bhikkhunī* applicants. Then an unexpected problem appeared. *Bhikkhunī* applicants with no such defects were intimidated at being questioned by a *Bhikku* and no longer wanted to pursue 'legal ordination'. So the Buddha ordered that *Bhikkhunī* applicants must

'Precept and Practice Seminar'
at the Geumgang Vinaya Seminary of Bongnyung-sa Temple (October 2015)

'Precept and Practice Seminar'
at the Geumgang Vinaya Seminary of Bongnyung-sa Temple

be approved by the *Bhikkhunī* order first and then by the *Bhikkus*."

- Culllavagga X

Therefore, the double ordination system was started to protect *Bhikkhunī* applicants from any discomfort at being questioned by a *Bhikku*. Now that we know why the double ordination system was started, I want to state that in my humble opinion, it is no longer necessary. Korean Buddhism, as a form of Mahāyāna Buddhism, should not stick to the Theravāda tradition that developed in India during the century after the Buddha passed away. The modern issue of gender equality needs to be addressed. Nevertheless, the Jogye Order still clings to this old tradition. What shall we do? That is why we need to listen to the voices of today's *Bhikkhunī*.

3

Bhikkhunīs in Buddhist History

1.
The *Bhikkhunīs*
the Buddha Praised

"Bhikkhus, the foremost of my bhikkhunī disciples in seniority is Mahāpajāpatī Gotamī."

"...among those with great wisdom is Khemā."

"...among those with psychic potency is Uppalavaṇṇā."

"...among those who uphold the discipline is Paṭācārā."

"...among speakers on the *Dhmma* is Dhmmadinnā."

"...among meditators is Nandā."

"...among those who arouse energy is Soṇā."

"...among those with the divine eye is Sakulā."

"...among those who quickly attain direct knowledge is Bhaddā Kuṇḍalakesā."

"...among those who recollect past lives is Bhaddā Kāpilānī."

"...among those who attain great direct knowledge is Bhaddā Kaccānā."

"...among those who wear coarse robes is Kisāgotamī."

"...among those resolved through faith is Sigālamātā."

- Aṅuttara Nikāa 1 「Foremost」 V

Becoming a terri (senior monk) and finally becoming a lotus (Buddha)...

III. *Bhikkhunīs* in Buddhist History

Since the Buddha first allowed women into the order, making the female monastic system possible, there have been many *Bhikkhunīs* who have attained 'the four accesses and four realizations' of the *sāvaka* path (四向四果), the path of Buddhist sainthood. We can easily confirm this fact, and they appear in early Buddhist scriptures, including Pali scriptures, in which the Buddha is unsparing in praising them. The Pāli scriptures mentioned above confirm the Buddha's praise for 13 *Bhikkhunīs* who were relatively prominent in the early days of Buddhism. Other outstanding qualities of *Bhikkhunīs* are also mentioned in several early Buddhist scriptures such as *Therigāthā* and the *Increased by One Āgama Suttas* (增一阿含經 Vol. 3, chapter on *Bhikkhunīs*). Ninety-two elder *Bhikkhunīs* mentioned in the *Therigāthā* attained *arahant*-ship, the stage in which all afflictions of the three realms have been permanently eliminated. In addition, 52 *Bhikkhunīs* are mentioned in the *Increased by One Āgama Suttas* (Vol. 3, chapter on *Bhikkhunīs*) which reveals their excellent talents in the areas of ascetic practice, insight, psychic power, and monastic discipline.

The Indian *Bhikkhunī* monastic order, after the death of the Buddha, constituted the axis of Buddhism and played a part in its continuous development and traditions. These records are not difficult to find in texts on Buddhist precepts, including *Vinaya of the Four Categories* (四分律). Furthermore, since the 3rd century BCE, female monastic orders have spread into Sri Lanka, Myanmar, China, Southeast Asia and Northeast Asia.

Currently, however, Theravada Buddhism and Tibetan Buddhism do not have a *Bhikkhunī* monastic order. That does not mean, however, that they have no *Bhikkhunīs*; they are simply not officially recognized. The reason for this is that the tradition of a *Bhikkhunī* monastic order was discontinued in early Theravada Buddhism. In Tibetan Buddhism, however, a *Bhikkhunī* monastic order never existed. That is because when Buddhism was first introduced to Tibet, the tradition of an Indian *Bhikkhunī* monastic order had already ended, and therefore, was never transmitted to Tibet.

On the other hand, there are still *Bhikkhunī* monastic orders in Korea, China and Taiwan. At present, the nations that give the highest status to *Bhikkhunīs* are Korea and Taiwan. The *Bhikkhunīs* of Korea and Taiwan are more numerous and have more influence than the female clergy of other religions in the world. In particular, Korean *Bhikkhunīs* are the only

The Buddha praised his excellent *Bhikkhunī* disciples often. Outstanding *Bhikkhunīs* can be found in scriptures such as the *Pali Canon, Verses of Elder Nuns* and *Increased by One Āgama Suttas.*

Theravāda Buddhism no longer recognizes *Bhikkhunīs*, but there are female practitioners called '*dasasilmātā*' who observe the 10 precepts received from a *Bhikkhu* preceptor.

ones to follow traditional Mahayana Buddhism, which is a great blessing to Korean *Bhikkhunīs*.

In accordance with King Asoka's policy (king of the Mauria dynasty, 268-232 BCE) of sending Buddhist missionaries to foreign lands, he sent his son Mahinda and his daughter Saṅghamittā to Sri Lanka to establish the *Bhikkhu* and *Bhikkhunī* orders. The Sri Lankan *Bhikkhunī* order became dynamically active and even dispatched ten male Buddhist masters to *Bhikkhunī* ordination ceremonies in China. However, after the Chola dynasty of southern India invaded Sri Lanka in the 11th century, the Buddhist order ceased to exist. The Sri Lankan *Bhikkhu* order was eventually restored and still thrives, but the *Bhikkhunī* order was not.

In the 5th century, Myanmar Buddhists welcomed Theravada Buddhism. Myanmar followed Esoteric Buddhism for a short period but reverted to Theravada Buddhism in the 11th century. For some time Buddhism in Myanmar was the only denomination in Southeast Asian Buddhism to recognize the *Bhikkhunī* order, but the order vanished in the 13th century and was never restored.

Thai Buddhists welcomed Theravada Buddhism from Myanmar some time after Esoteric Buddhism was first introduced to Thailand around the 8th century and welcomed Sri Lankan Theravada Buddhism at the end of the 13th century. Buddhism in Cambodia and Laos dates back to the 13th century. They adopted Thailand's Theravada Buddhism after they were invaded by Thailand, however, there has never been a *Bhikkhunī* order in any of those three countries. As a result, the Buddhist community in Southeast Asia no longer has a *Bhikkhunī* monastic order because they can not have two forms of ordination ceremonies for both a male and female order. However, there are renunciant female practitioners called '*dasasilmātā*' who observe the ten precepts they receive from a *Bhikkhu* (male) preceptor.

The Buddhist community is called the *saṅgha* (僧伽) and consists of four distinct groups which were codified at the time of the Buddha as the four assemblies (四部大衆): female and male clergy and female and male laity. This indicates a long tradition of egalitarian and democratic ideals which form the social and political structure of Buddhism. However, unlike the Buddha, who advocated and practiced the gender equality within the limitations of his time, later Buddhist institutions were corroded by a patriarchal society and the cultures in which these institutions were formed. Korea was no exception, and female monks suffered greatly, specifically because they were women. However, the environment for female Buddhist clergy in Korea has changed rapidly in the past 30 years. Nuns now occupy a crucial position in the modern Jogye order, the largest Buddhist denomination in Korea, and rival monks in terms of importance, even though this is not always acknowledged.

Like male monks, female monks receive full ordination, a practice which today is only found in Korea and Taiwan. Not only does the total number of nuns almost equal the number of monks, *Bhikkhunīs* are active participants in the Buddhist tradition in various capacities such as: avid meditators, compassionate caretakers for the needy, adept administrators of social welfare facilities, and attentive and powerful leaders of city-based Buddhist centers. They are also ardent activists who demand democracy and oppose prejudice, both within the Jogye Order and in the broader society as well. Korean nuns have built a viable monastic community that has survived near obliteration and established its own power of regeneration. This is reflected in its continual growth, its social activism, and its meditation programs, and it makes the Korean *Bhikkhunī* monastic order one of the most vibrant and formidable female monastic communities in the modern religious world.

Through an examination of historical records and biographical excerpts by Buddhist nuns, we can see that Korean *Bhikkhunīs* have maintained a tradition of religious practice and commitment to the *Dhamma* from the very inception of Buddhism in Korea. With a long history of 1,600 years, Korean *Bhikkhunīs* stand out in the history of world religion. The accepted theory today holds that when the male monastic order was formed after Buddhism arrived in Korea, a *Bhikkhunī* order was established at almost the same time. It is a well known fact that nuns from the Baekje Kingdom went to Japan and played a decisive role in the establishment of a *Bhikkhunī* order in Japan. At present, of all the Buddhist countries, Korea and Taiwan are the first among the East Asian Mahayana Buddhist countries that maintains a Buddhist order of female monks with full precepts.

Moreover, when we take into account its long history, the status of Korea's *Bhikkhunī* tradition is very significant. They have now built a viable monastic community that has not only survived near-obliteration during the Joseon era and afterward, but continues to flourish and develop, reflected in the order's continuing growth, its social activism, and its meditation programs, making it one of the most flourishing female monastic communities in the modern Buddhist world.

2.
The Transmission of Buddhism to Korea and the First Korean *Bhikkhunīs*

Ado (阿道) proceeded to the palace and propagated Buddhist teachings there, but there had been people before who doubted the teachings and had even tried to kill him. So Ado ran away and hid in the house of Morye (毛禮). In the third year of King Michu's reign, Princess Sungguk became sick. The king tried to cure her with sorcery and medicines, but they did not work. Ado heard this and visited the palace without hesitation to cure the princess, which he did. The king was very pleased and offered Ado whatever he wanted. Ado replied.

"I do not want anything. I just want to build Buddhist temples in Cheongyung Forest (天鏡林) and pray for the blessing of the country."

The king allowed it. A temple was constructed, and Ado propagated the Buddha's teaching there. That temple was Heungryun-sa. Morae's sister, Lady Sa, became a Buddhist nun under the guidance of Ado and built a temple in the Sacheonggi area. That temple was Youngheung-sa.

- *Samguk Yusa* Vol. 3 Heungbeop 3, Adogira (阿道基羅)

Master Ado is a monk before and a teacher of Lady Sa (史氏), the first female monk in Korea. This bronze statue is housed in Dori-sa Temple at Seonsan county in Gyeongbuk Province.

The sitting meditation pedestal on which Master Ado sat
(Dori-sa Temple in Seonsan county)

The official date of Buddhism's arrival in Korea is the second year (372) of the reign of Goguryeo's 17th king, Sosurim. This date is based on the *Samguk sagi* (三國史記 *History of the Three Kingdoms*) which says:

"In 372, when King Sosurim of Goguryeo (高句麗) was crowned, King Fujian (符堅) (338-385) of Jin (晉) China sent to Goguryeo many Buddhist statues and scriptures written by the Buddhist monk Shun-tao (順道). In 374, the monk Ado (阿道) came from Eastern Jin (東晉) to propagate Buddhism and built many temples. This was the beginning of the Buddha's teachings in the Goguryeo Kingdom."

- Samguk Sagi Vol.18

Another Korean text, the *Samguk Yusa* (三國遺事 *Legends and History of the Three Kingdoms*), confirms this. To be more precise, 372 may not be the actual year Buddhism arrived, but it is the earliest year found in existing records. Twelve years later in 384 (the first year of the reign of Baekje's King Chimnyu), the monk Mālânanda from Serindia (modern Xinjiang Province) arrived in Baekje (百濟) after traveling in Eastern Jin (東晉) and began transmitting Buddhist teachings. In 527 during the reign of Silla's King Beopheung (法興王), Buddhism became the official state religion of Silla after the martyrdom of I Chadon (503–527), who had strongly advocated for it. He was executed for his activities. These are the earliest official records of Buddhism in the Three Kingdoms period.

This is the well at Morye's house where Master Ado hid and continued to propagate Buddhism. Morye was a lay Buddhist who provided Ado a place to stay when Buddhism was first introduced to Silla. Morye's sister, Lady Sa, was the first female monk in Korea.

However, according to the *Samguk Yusa* (三國遺事 *Legends* and *History of the Three Kingdoms* Vol.3 Heungbeop 興法), in the year 263 during the reign of King Michu of Goguryo (高句麗), the monk Ado came to Silla to propagate Buddhism. This was more than 100 years before what is thought to be the year Buddhism first arrived in Korea. Ado stayed at Eumjang-sa (嚴莊寺) on the western side of the palace. He tried to propagate Buddhism, but the people tried to kill him because they were suspicious of a religion they had never heard of before. Ado hid in the house of Morye (毛禮), a female lay Buddhist, in Soklim in Ilseon County (present day Seonsan-gun in Gyeongbuk Province). The following year, after curing the princess of an ailment, he built Heungryun-sa Temple and continued teaching Buddhism. After King Michu died, Ado again hid in Morye's house to avoid being hurt, where he later died, and Buddha's teachings along with him.

Regarding the influx of Buddhism into the Silla Dynasty, it is very interesting to note that Ado was hidden by Morye, a female lay Buddhist who provided him a place to stay when Buddhism was first introduced to Silla. Therefore, her house can be considered the first foundation for Buddhist missionary work carried out before Buddhism was even made the official state religion of Silla.

There is also historical significance to the name Morye because it was her sister, Lady Sa (史氏), who became the first Korean female known to have renounced the secular world to become a Buddhist nun. The quote at the beginning of this section confirms this. This is the first known record of such an event in Korea. According to the record, Lady Sa became a female monk by virtue of her acquaintance with Ado, and

The royal tomb of King Beopheung (法興王) of Silla. His queen was the first official Korean female monk who took the *Dhamma* name Myobeop (妙法).

she later founded Yeongheung-sa.

Silla's King Beopheung (法興王 r. 514-540) and his wife converted to Buddhism after it became the official state religion in 527. In 540, King Beopheung renounced the throne and became a monk, and his queen (*Dhamma* name Myobeop 妙法) became a nun, "out of respect for Lady Sa's path." However, Lady Sa and the queen could not have received official ordination.

Women were only allowed to become Buddhist nuns after a decree was issued to that effect in 544, the fifth year of King Jinheung's reign (眞興王 r. 540-576), King Beopheung's successor. According to another event in *Samguk sagi* (三國史記 *History of the Three Kingdoms*), King Jinheung's Queen

Sadobuin (思刀夫人) and Kim Yu-sin's wife, Jisobuin (智炤夫人) also had their hair cut to become Buddhist nuns. However, because Lady Sa's renunciation occurred much earlier than the year the decree was issued, her renunciation cannot be recognized as official. It was only her personal decision. On the other hand, it is true that some academics recognize King Beopheung's queen, Myobeop, as the first official Buddhist nun in Korean history.

Despite the paucity of historical material, it is generally agreed that the Korean female monastic order was established at almost the same time as the monks', that being when Buddhism first arrived in Korea. The two seminal historic resources for ancient Korea are the *Samguk yusa* (三國遺事 *Legends and History of the Three Kingdoms*, written by the Goryeo monk Iryeon 一然) and the *Samguk sagi* (*History of the Three Kingdoms*, compiled in 1145 by Kim Pusik and others). Both contain records of Buddhist nuns and female lay practitioners, proving the existence of Korean nuns from the very beginning of Buddhism in Korea some 1,600 years ago.

3.
Some Prominent *Bhikkhunīs* in Korean History

1) Ancient Times: The Three Kingdoms Period

The title *guktong* (國統) was given to the monk who served as the overall general supervisor for monks and nuns of the *saṅgha*. In the 12th year (551) of the reign of Silla's King Jinheung (眞興王), Master Hyerang (惠亮法師) of Goguryeo was appointed *guktong*, and the Buddhist nun Ani was appointed *doyunarang* (都唯那娘), controller of all female monasteries. Master Boryang (寶良法師) was appointed as *daedoyuna* (大都唯那) who was in charge of *Bhikkhus* as a whole for the first time during King Jinheung's period. The title *daeseosung* (大書省) was given to the royal Buddhist adviser, and during the reign of King Jinheung, that title was given to Master Anjang (安藏法師). In the third year (787) of the reign of King Wonseong (元聖王), the two *Dhamma* teachers Hyeyoung (惠英) and Beomyeo (梵如) were appointed *sonyeonseosung* (少年書省) which translates as 'young advisor'.

- Samguk Sagi (三國史記) Vol. 40

As previously stated, in the early days of Buddhism in Korea, Lady Sa (史氏) was the first female renunciant, and King Beopheung's (法興王 r. 514-540) queen became the first officially recognized Buddhist nun, taking the *Dhamma* name Myobeop (妙法). Sometime later, the wives of both King Jinheung (眞興王 r. 540–576) and General Kim Yu-sin (金庾信 595-673) of the Silla Dynasty also became Buddhist nuns.

Korea's other kingdoms also used a system of official monastic positions. Goguryeo appointed a *seungtong* (僧統, monk superintendent), Korea's other kingdoms also used a system of official monastic positions. and Baekje appointed a *seungjeong* (僧正, rector of monks). Silla also established the position of *seunggwan* (僧官, director of monks). It is interesting to note that the nun Ani was eventually appointed to this position which gave her more authority than male monks. The above information from the *Samguk Sagi* Vol. 40 is valuable evidence that confirms the status of Buddhist nuns at that time. During the reign of Silla's 26th king, Jinpyeong (眞平王 579 ~ 632), the name Jihye (智惠) is also mentioned, a Buddhist nun who worked hard and received much praise.

According to the existing Japanese records such as *Nihon*

A statute of Mālânanda (摩羅難陀), a Serindian monk who traveled to Eastern Jin and later to Baekje, transmitting the Buddhist teachings. This statute is located at Buyong-lu Pavilion in Beopsung-po, Younggwang Jeollanam-do Province where Buddhism first arrived. Baekje Buddhism directly influenced Japanese Buddhism.

shoki (日本書紀 Chronicles of Japan) and others, we can see the active missionary activities of Baekje (百濟) *Bhikkhunīs* in Japan. Many Japanese records confirm that King Seong-wang (r. 523-554) of Baekje transmitted Buddhism to Japan in 538 for the first time in Japanese history. The first record of Baekje nuns comes from *Nihon Shoki* which states that Baekje sent Buddhist missionaries, including a nun, to Japan in 577. It is known that Baekje regularly dispatched Buddhist doctrinal specialists, iconographers, and architects to Japan over well-traveled sea lanes, thus transmitting the rudiments

Ⅲ. *Bhikkhunīs* in Buddhist History

of Sino-Korean Buddhist culture and laying the foundation for the rich Buddhist culture of Japan's Asuka (飛鳥) and Nara periods (奈良).

Nihon Shoki also says that a Baekje nun named Beopmyong (法明) went to Tsushima Island in 655 and cured a high Japanese official of an ailment by reciting the *Vimalakīrti-nirdeśa-sūtra* (維摩經). Another Baekje nun named Beopmyo (法妙) founded Shuzen–ji Temple (修善寺) on Tsushima Island. It is noteworthy that Baekje Buddhism had two separate ordination systems, one for males and one for females. This means that Baekje's female Buddhist order was an established Buddhist community that had influence in the religious community. The Baekje Buddhist community (both males and females) worked together in a common effort to attain Buddhahood.

According to the Japanese record, a *Bhikkhunī* named Yi-won (理願) of Silla Kingdom built a temple in the Japanese mansion, called Daiban Anma, located at the foot of Mt. Jungbo in Nara, Japan, and worked hard for 30 years missionary in Japan. In 735, she passed away.

2) Medieval Times: The Goryeo Dynasty

The history of female Buddhist monks during the Goryeo Dynasty and their activities is revealed in various sources just as it was in the Three Kingdoms period. Together with such official historical records as *Goryeosa* (高麗史, History of Goryeo) and *Goryeosa Jeolyo* (高麗史節要, Essentials of Goryeo History), we find evidence in epigraphs, collections of literary works and memorial inscriptions.

As we all know, the Goryeo Dynasty embraced a form of nationalistic Buddhism, meaning that the ordination process was controlled by the state. In the ninth year of the reign of King Gwanjong (光宗), a state examination system for Buddhist monks was introduced at the recommendation of Chinese government officials, and Goryeo state control was applied equally to all monks, both male and female.

Hyewon (慧圓, 851-938) was the first Buddhist nun to be ordained during the Goryeo Dynasty, a period of nationalistic Buddhism. According to one source, she was also the first abbess of Cheongnyong-sa (靑龍寺), which was established as a royal temple in 922. The nuns Manseon (萬善 996-1060) and

Jihwan (知幻 1261-1312), who reconstructed Cheongnyong-sa Temple, were ordained after Hyewon.

Goryeo had one main capital (Gaegyeong 開京) and three secondary capitals (Seogyeong, Donggyeong and Namgyeong). The two temples Daeseowon (大西院, Big School) and Soseowon (小西院, Small School) in Seogyeong (西京), Goryeo's western capital and present day Pyongyang (平壤), were managed by two Buddhist nuns with the titles of Lady Daeseowon (大西院夫人) and Lady Soseowon (小西院夫人) in the early Goryeo period (高麗 918-1392). They were the two daughters of a powerful local family clan called the Kim Haeng-pa in the western capital, which was elevated to the capital in 922 by King Taejo Wangeun.

At first, the two daughters served King Taejo as their father wished, but when King Taejo ceased visiting them in Seogyeong, they became Buddhist nuns to maintain their chastity. When King Taejo heard this, he took pity on them and granted them two temples along with land and farmers to work the land. Historical documents refer to them as King Taejo's 'Queen 19' and 'Queen 20'.

According to Master Bojo Jinul's (普照知訥, 1158~1210) '*Samādhi* and *Paññā* Society' (定慧結社) at Suseon-sa Temple (now Songgwang-sa Temple 松廣寺 on Mt. Jogye 曹溪山), there is a list of Buddhist nuns who participated in summer retreats there. They include: Jongmin (宗敏), Cheongwon (清遠), Huiwon (希遠) and Yoyeon (了然). *Bhikkhunī* Cheonghye's (清惠) name is mentioned at Anyang-sa Temple in 1252. *Bhikkhunī* Moi (某伊) oversaw a project to complete a sutta painting titled *Gwangyeong-sipyukgwan-byunsangdo* at Naksan-sa Temple in northwestern Gyeonggi Province (京畿道).

There is the only person who received the *Dhamma* precept, 'Great Teacher (大師)' as a *Bhikkhunī* of the Goryeo Dynasty. She was Seong-hyo (性曉 1255-1324). When Seong-hyo passed away, the King Choongsook gave her a posthumous title as "Byunhanguk Daebuin Jinhye Great Teacher (卞韓國大夫人 眞慧 大師)". Seong-hyo was the wife, Lady Huo of Kim Byun (金骈 1248-1301), who served as a member of the retinue to the China. Later Kim Byun was installed as a second rate meritorious retainer. Lady Huo's husband died at the age of 47, and she left her footsteps as *Bhikkhunī* for 10 years after enlightenment ordination in 1315 (the 2nd year of King Choongsook) at the age of 61. She was the only *Bhikkhunī* in the Goryeo period who received the posthumous title.

Wonjeungguksa Taego Bou Bimun (Master Taego Bou's epigraph)
Master Taego Bou's female disciple monks are mentioned in this inscription.

The ordination of Buddhist nuns ended in late Goryeo. This fact is evident by the lists of Buddhist nuns engraved in the inscriptions of great masters. One inscription titled *Wonjeung Guksa Tapbimun*, found at Taego-sa Temple on Mt. Bukhan-san, mentions one Buddhist nun, a follower of Taego Bo-u (太古普愚, 1301~1382) named Myoan (妙安).

Another inscription titled *Bojeseonsa-seokjong-bimun*, located at Silleuk-sa Temple (神勒寺), contains the names of many female followers (*Bhikkhunīs*) of Naong Hyegeun (懶翁慧勤, 1320~1376). These include: Ven. Myobong (妙峯) (abbess of Jeungeup-won Temple [淨業院]), Myodeuk (妙德), Myogan (妙玕), Myosin (妙信), Myohae (妙海), Myohye (妙惠), Myojung (妙重), Myoheun (妙憲), Myohyun (妙玄), Myogyung (妙瓊), Myoin (妙因), Myojin (妙珍), Myoryung (妙玲), Myohan (妙閑), Weolmee (月眉) , Myojing (妙澄), Myochong (妙摠), Myodang (妙幢), Myoeung (妙應) and Ven. Myoseon (妙善).

Among these *Bhikkhunīs*, Myochong (妙摠) left behind a hymn of enlightenment, and Myodeuk (妙德) arranged the financing to publish Master Baekun Gyeonghan's *Collected Writings of Baekun and Essential Passages that Directly Point at the Essence of the Mind* (直指心體要節). The latter was

Bojeseonsa Sariseokjong Bimun (Master Boje's epigraph) at Silleuk-sa Temple in Yeoju-gun, Gyeonggi-do Province. In this inscription, the names of 200 of Master Naong Hyegeun's (1320–1376 a Goryeo Seon monk) followers appear.

designated as a Memory of the World Heritage by UNESCO in 2001 because it was the first ever text printed using moveable metal-type in 1377, predating the Gutenberg Bible by 78 years.

Cases of females becoming Buddhist nuns in the Goryeo period (高麗 918-1392) can be confirmed by epitaphs, also known as memorial inscriptions. According to the text Collection of Goryeo Dynasty Epitaphs (高麗墓誌銘集成), Lady Choi (1227-1309), the wife of a civil servant named Kim Gu (金坵, 1211~1278), lived alone for 30 years after her husband died.

Just one day before her death at the age of 83, she became a Buddhist nun and received the *Dhamma* name Hyangjin (向眞, lit. 'toward truth'). Another female known as Lady Park (1249~1318), who lived at about the same time, was the wife of a civil servant named Choi Seo (崔瑞, 1233~1305). She received the precepts and became a Buddhist nun immediately before her death after receiving the *Dhamma* name Sunggong (省空, lit. 'retrospection of emptiness'). She also chanted and recited the names of Amitâbha Buddha at the time of her death.

The community life of Buddhist nuns in the Goryeo period was mainly centered on Jeongeup-won (淨業院) and Anil-won (安逸院) Temples. These temples for Buddhist nuns were mainly centers of activity for nuns from the royal and ruling classes. According to *History of Goryeo* Vol. 18 (世家), they were already established in 1164 in the capital city Gaeseong (開成). Even during the Mongolian invasion when the Goryeo capital was moved to Ganghwa-do Island, Jeongeup-won continued to provide 'a certain amount of space' for Buddhist nuns to stay in the castle in Gaeseong; 'a certain amount of space' means that the military government designated the house of Park Hwon (朴暄, died in 1249) as Jeongeup-won Temple after his death.

Even in times of turmoil, Jeongeup-won Temple was reserved for nuns. The fact that Anil-won Temple was a temple for nuns was first recorded in 1383 (9th year of the reign of King U-wang) in *History of Goryeo* (Vol. 18. separate biographies 列傳 48). Goryeo's Anil-won and Jeongeup-won Temples survived until the late Joseon Dynasty.

Other historic records provide more interesting facts about the Goryeo era; they deal with a state ban on female renunciants. Most of the Goryeo era data on Buddhist nuns deals with state-imposed prohibitions and/or regulations. They state that a total of three bans on female renunciation were announced during the Goryeo Dynasty.

These bans were announced: in January 1017 by King Hyeonjong (顯宗 8), in December 1359 by King Gongmin (恭愍王 8) and in December 1388 by King Changgwang (昌王 18). These were times of war and social chaos, including several invasions from China. In particular, during the reign of King Hyeonjong, only women were banned from becoming monks because wars were more severe than ever due to a series of invasions by the Khitans (1st in 993, 2nd in 1010, 3rd in 1018). Another reason for the ban was that many women chose to become nuns as a form of mourning after losing their husbands in war. This phenomenon, which appears to have increased rapidly in periods of social chaos and isolation, is very interesting even from today's perspective.

There is one more thing to note about the activities of nuns in the Goryeo Dynasty. Buddhist nuns from the lower and oppressed classes generally lived scattered throughout the country, and as a result, they escaped much of the state control that was imposed on nuns from the royal and ruling classes. By the end of the Goryeo era there were even cases of male and female monks living together as couples. This violation of the precepts was behind many of the regulations imposed on monks and nuns at the national level. Nevertheless, in spite of the state-imposed ban on females becoming ordained, there were still many female renunciants. This might have been due to the influence of social chaos, or it might have had something to do with society's feelings toward nationalistic Buddhism. Considering the various regulations and restrictions imposed by Goryeo officials, the unremitting efforts of *Bhikkhunīs* to persevere were a firm foundation to guarantee the permanence of a female Buddhist order today and into the future.

In Goryeo, King Taejo (太祖) declared Buddhism as the state religion, providing a momentum for its spread. According to the *History of Goryeo* (高麗史), however, it seems that the position of nuns during this period was not any higher than in the Three Kingdoms and United Silla eras. Becoming a monk served as a means for social rise in Goryeo, but becoming a *Bhikkhunī* appears to have been a solution to overcome personal misfortunes in life more or less.

3) Modern Times: The Joseon Dynasty

> As this body has been tainted with much dust,
> even the blue mountain doesn't like me.
> Even though the heavens and earth are wide,
> there is no place to rely upon.
> How can the royal inspector catch this drifting body?

> *- Dongpyeongwui-Gongsa-Kyeonmoonrok* (東平尉公私見聞錄)

This is a poem titled "Lamenting Oneself", written by a *bhikkhunī* named Yesun (Dhamma name 禮順, 1587~1657) who lived in the mid-Joseon Dynasty. Her original name was Yeosun or Youngil. This poem may simply be the product of a strong will, but it is also sad because it depicts the regrets of a *bhikkhunī* entangled in the politics of that era.

Yesun was a mere Buddhist nun who left a clear mark in the Joseon Dynasty. She was the eldest daughter of Lee Gui (李貴, 1557 ~ 1633) who, along with her father, played a major role in King Injo's 'Restoration of the Rectitude' in 1623. This was a political incident that led to the overthrow of King Gwanghae-gun by a faction of Westerners and the enthronement of King Injo (仁祖). However, Yesun suffered for this incident later in life. That incident was the result of political factionalism and endless human greed that was rife in the Joseon Dynasty (朝鮮 1392–1910).

Yesun's poem depicts her situation at the time, an era tainted with insatiable human desire. The term "tainted with much dust" refers to her being unable to escape from secular desires even though she had already renounced the secular world and become a nun. As a result of helping her father and betraying her acquaintance Kim Gyesi (a palace attendant), many lives were lost. That is why she felt her body was tainted with the dust of this world. Therefore, the poem's message is that people who are enmeshed in the worldly life and harbor worthless desires cannot live on "the blue mountain" (i.e. in nature). After her renunciation, she thought she could live among nature. However, the poem indicates she seems to dislike herself for not being able to avoid such worldly matters as revolts and killing.

Yesun was born named as Yeosun (女順) or Yeongil (英日) and was married to Kim Jagyeom (金自謙), a younger brother of Kim Jajeom who played a key role in the Injo Coup. While married, Yeosun and her husband devoted themselves to Buddhism, but her husband died at the age of 20. He left a will saying she should continue to study Buddhism with his friend Oh Eon-gwan (吳彦寬, ?~1614), who was also a devout Buddhist. In accordance with her husband's will, she was often taught by Oh Eon-gwan and discussed Buddhism with him. Eventually, Yeosun attained an intuitive knowledge of the minds of all other beings, a supernatural ability to read the minds of others. She was so famous that even Queen Yu, King Gwanghae-gun's wife, and many other people regarded her as a 'living Buddha', a term of respect for an eminent living monk. Ultimately, she entered the Buddhist order. At the age of 24, she received the *Dhamma* name Yesun from her teacher Dosim (道心) at Cheongyong-sa Temple in Seoul.

In March 1623, the Injo Coup plot was discovered, and her father and half of the plotters were in danger of being arrested.

Yesun then sent a letter to her acquaintance, Kim Gyesi, and told him her father was being framed. After receiving her letter and a poem of loyalty to King Gwanghae-gun, Kim Gyesi believed her and persuaded the king to withdraw the arrest warrant. Unfortunately, it was too late.

Afterward, she returned to Cheongyong-sa Temple and served as its abbess. She later renovated Cheongyong-sa Temple and performed rituals for those who had died in the coup. One of those was Prince Youngchang Daegun, another victim of factional strife. After suffering through the Manchu Invasion of December 1636 (the 14th year of the reign of King Injo), she returned to Cheongyong-sa Temple. She supported the temple by practicing Buddhism and teaching Buddhism many people. In 1657 (the 8th year of King Hyojong's reign), she died at the age of 71. She lived a turbulent and stormy life and spent much of her life repenting for the anguish she had caused, stuck between the Buddha's realm and the mundane world.

The Joseon dynasty, which succeeded Goryeo, adopted an anti-Buddhist policy during its early stages. However, its enforcement was not consistent as is seen during the reign of King Taejong (太宗 1401-1418) and also during the later years of King Sejong's (世宗 1418-1450) rule. The Joseon court legally forbade womens' renunciation. Although King Sejo (世祖) reversed the anti-Buddhist policy and permitted women to become nuns as a way of promoting Buddhism, the court resumed the oppression of the Buddhist community from the mid-Joseon period while reinforcing its support for Confucianism. The Jogye Order of Korean Buddhism was established at the end of the Japanese occupation period, and with this, a *Bhikkhunī* ordination was revived in Korea. Thus, it is after 1900 that the full-scale training and ordination of *Bhikkhunīs* began in the modern era.

The Joseon Dynasty was a period when neo-Confucianism dominated, and Buddhism, which had shaped Korean culture throughout the previous dynasties, was suppressed. By adopting the official policy of promoting Confucianism and repressing Buddhism, the government strictly excluded as heretics those who didn't follow neo-Confucianism. This was the main defining characteristic of the Joseon Dynasty. In the late Joseon Dynasty, there was a level of class discrimination not seen in previous times. This was a time when the inequality between nobles and commoners reached extreme levels, and four distinct classes of society were recognized: scholars, farmers, artisans and tradesmen (士農工商). Women suffered the most at this time because neo-Confucianism was a male-dominated ideology that not only made clear distinctions between the roles of men and women but also viewed women as inferior to men (男尊女卑). This was a second major characteristic of the Joseon Dynasty.

Of course, there were many other issues that defined Joseon: subservience to authority, political strife and strong class distinctions. However, as it relates to this book, I must also include the suppression of Buddhism and gender discrimination. The dominance of neo-Confucianism in Joseon appears to have created a strong gender bias in Joseon Buddhism.

The history of Joseon Buddhism was mostly stable but also saw some extreme changes. The founders and most officials of the new Joseon Dynasty were neo-Confucians who oppressed Buddhism and encouraged Confucianism (崇儒斥佛). Their policies and laws were extremely ani-Buddhist and oppressive to monks (排佛抑僧). This was true from the very start of the Joseon Dynasty. Buddhists endured systematic persecution from both government and civil society. It was a low point for all Buddhist monks and their devotees in Korea. Many Buddhist sects were merged to make them easier for the government to control. The state examination system that allowed people to officially become certified monks was abolished, and monks and nuns were also banned from entering the capital.

The repression of Buddhism during Joseon's 500-year history can be compared to the repression of Buddhism by Puṣhyamitra Sunga, founder of India's Sunga Dynasty (187-78 BCE) and one of the most brutal anti-Buddhist rulers in history. Four other brutal anti-Buddhist Chinese emperors are known collectively as the "three Wu and one Zong Emperors" (三武一宗法難). In order to survive the Joseon Dynasty, many Buddhist monks retreated to the mountains, and that is why today most of Korea's Buddhist temples are located deep in the mountains. The oppression of Buddhism by Joseon leaders lasted until about 1895 when the ban against Buddhist monks entering the capital was lifted.

In spite of the oppression, Buddhism did not entirely disappear in Joseon Korea. Even though many government officials and members of the royal family publically condemned Buddhism as superstition and heresy, they could not entirely eliminate it. The royal court still followed certain Goryeo Buddhist practices, and the gentry could not entirely abandon certain traditional Buddhist rites. Even though the government officially opposed Buddhism, the common people and even the royal family could not escape its cultural and social influence which had shaped Korean society for centuries. Buddhism was still alive beneath the surface.

Some Buddhist activities pursued by the royal family were the building of altars called *wondang* (願堂, royal shrine) within the palace or inner Buddha halls (內願堂). It was originally a Goryeo custom where portraits of ancestors were enshrined.

However, these inner Buddha halls were not always located in the palace. At the time of Queen Munjeong, who led the Buddhist revival in Joseon, more than 300 Buddhist temples across the country were designated inner Buddha halls and supported by the royal family. When parents of nobility died, their descendants called in Buddhist monks to perform a funeral ceremony. Even in early Joseon, when anti-Buddhist sentiment was very strong, Confucians secretly held a Buddhist funeral or memorial service for their parents.

What is more important is that there were certain groups who continued to practice Buddhism even in early Joseon. They were usually females of the royal family, or so-called 'Confucian family women' who set up Buddhist temples or altars in the palace to continue their Buddhist activities. They were usually women or concubines left behind after a king, queen or other member died for whatever reason, often treason or betrayal. It was the custom for a concubine and her attendants to stay on in the palace after a king or other family member died, and it was often common for them to become Buddhist nuns. Even if a concubine did not become a nun, she might set up a Buddhist shrine or altar in the palace and attend a Buddhist service in the morning and evening.

The royal court was originally established as a residence for royal wives, but all the women who entered the palace practiced Buddhism. So the royal palace gradually turned into a form of *Bhikkhunī* temple with names like Jasuwon (慈壽院) and Insuwon (仁壽院). These *Bhikkhunī* temples were regarded as sites for the revival of Buddhist nuns in Joseon. At the time of Queen Munjeong, more than 5,000 *Bhikkhunīs* practiced in the palace, and this period was considered a golden age for *Bhikkhunīs* in Joseon. Many royal palaces were burnt down during the Japanese invasion of Korea in 1592, but one royal *Bhikkhunī* temple survived near newly-constructed Changdeok-gung Palace. In addition to Jasuwon and Insuwon, there were two other *Bhikkhunī* temples that had been established in Goryeo, Jeongup-won and Anil-won.

There were many places for *Bhikkhunīs* to practice in Joseon, including the palace temples and four Buddhist nunneries which were collectively called the *sa-seungbang* (四僧房). These were: Saejeol Seongbang on Mt. Samgak-san at Cheongnyong-sa Temple, Tapgol Seongbang at Bomoon-sa Temple, Dumuggye Seongbang on Mt. Jongnam-san at Mita-sa Temple, and Dolgoji Seongbang on Mt. Chunjang-san at Seokgo-sa Temple. However, these centers of *Bhikkhunī* activity suffered a series of setbacks in Joseon when they were abolished by Confucian officials. In 1475 (the 6th year of King Sungjong' s reign) 23 Buddhist temples near the capital were closed due to strong opposition by Confucian scholars. At that time, the royal court officially allowed only the four Buddhist nunneries mentioned above to remain active.

In 1623 (the first year of King Injo' s reign) a total ban on Buddhist monks entering the capital was imposed. In 1661 (the second year of King Hyunjong's reign) women of the royal family were no longer allowed to become nuns, and the *Bhikkhunī* temples of Jasuwon and Insuwon were closed. From that time on, no activity by nuns was officially sanctioned in the palace, and the Buddhist traditions of Goryeo disappeared. Beginning in latter Joseon, followers of Buddhism became more interested in seeking good fortune than in seeking truth, and women of the royal court began to prefer having sons more than retreating to a nunnery. However, the desire to have a son was so popular that many women visited temples to pray for a son.

The popular versions of stories about women of royalty and the wives of Confucians becoming Buddhist nuns are often quite different from the actual facts. People often say these women renounced the secular world after a broken heart or a loved one's death or something along those lines. Even so, it was their choice to have their heads shaved, dye their clothing and become a Buddhist nun. Actually, for a lady of the royal court, it was the only way to preserve her chastity and live as an independent personality.

According to the book *Hansagyung* about the rise and fall

Cheongnyong-sa Temple on Mt. Samgaksan, constructed by King Taejo of Goryeo as a *Bhikkhunī* Temple.

Tapgol Seungbang Bomun-sa Temple, one of four Buddhist nunneries (seungbang 僧房) recognized officially by the government.

Mita-sa Temple on Mt. Jongnam-san, recognized officially as one of Korea's four Buddhist nunneries.

Cheongryang-sa Temple on Mt. Chunjang-san. One of four Buddhist nunneries recognized officially by the government.

III. *Bhikkhunīs* in Buddhist History

of the Joseon Dynasty, when Danjong (the 6th king of Joseon) was dethroned and exiled to Gangneung, Shin Sook-ju, a high government official, asked the newly-crowned King Sejo to give him Danjong's queen. At that time, it was easy for a noble to turn a woman into a slave if they wished. Therefore, becoming a nun was often preferable.

Even though Joseon Buddhism was severely oppressed by the dominant neo-Confucian ideology, it did not entirely disappear. The Buddhist nuns of Jeoseon were no different from the divine guardians who defend the Buddha-*Dhamma*. They were the unsung heroes who sacrificed themselves to preserve Buddhism in a hostile environment.

Beginning in the latter part of the Joseon Dynasty, court women, common women and even the nobility began visiting temples to study Buddha's teachings. Although the *Bhikkhunī* order disappeared after the mid-17th century, its dynamism, formerly seen in royal Buddhist temples, lived on and was reformed by the royal family's unofficial, private respect for Buddhism, their continuing to practice Buddhism, and their protection of temples.

During this period of enlightenment, scenes of several

temples caught the eye of Isabella Bird Bishop (1832-1904), an English writer and geographer, and she provides us a glimpse of the Buddhist order in late Joseon. Her book *Korea and Her Neighbors* (1898) tells us the following about Korea's Geumgang-san (金剛山) Mountain region:

"In the nun's dormitory of Jangan-sa Temple lived around 100~120 Buddhist nuns, one 87-year-old and many novice nuns. Together at Yujeum-sa Temple lived around 70 male monks and 20 Buddhist nuns."

Her book describes in brief the political, economic and social situation as well as the culture and customs of Joseon, from the royal family to the poor, as she witnessed it from February 1894 to 1897.

One social phenomenon that cannot be overlooked in latter Joseon was the strengthening of clan blood ties, which did not exist in previous eras. In Silla and Goryeo, sons and sons-in-law formed almost a single cohesive group, and property was equally inherited by sons and daughters.

This social phenomenon penetrated Joseon Buddhism as well, and *Bhikkhus* discriminating against *Bhikkhunīs* became the norm, which the nuns accepted as natural. In general, Korean *Bhikkhunīs* seem to conform to discrimination

III. *Bhikkhunīs* in Buddhist History

without much opposition.

British philosopher John Stuart Mill (1806-1873) said, "All men, except the most brutish, desire to have, in the woman most nearly connected with them, not a forced slave but a willing one...." And Simone de Beauvoir (1908-1986), a contemporary female French writer and philosopher, said, "One is not born a woman but becomes one." These are wise sayings about how discrimination against women begins and how it spreads.

From here on I want to review those *Bhikkhunīs* who left their mark in Korean history during the difficult times of the Joseon Dynasty when Buddhism was oppressed Buddhism and Confucianism promoted.

In this difficult period the first woman to renounce the secular world was Princess Gyeong-soon, the third daughter of King Taejo, born Yi Seonggye. Gyeong-soon was the younger sister of Prince Muan Daegun. According to Annals of the Joseon Dynasty, Princess Gyeong-soon was married to Yi Je (李濟, 1365-1398). In August 1398, her husband and two younger brothers, Princes Bangbeon and Bangseok, were murdered by her other brother, Prince Bangwon. The following year, King Taejo had her become a Buddhist nun, and she stayed at Jeongup-won Temple.

Prince Bangseok's wife, Mrs. Shim, became the first *Bhikkhunī* during a power struggle now called "First Strife of the Princess." She was later appointed abbess of Jeongeup-won Temple in February 1408. The elder sister of Queen Jeong－an (King Jeongjong' s wife), Lady Kim was also appointed abbess of Jeongup-won Temple in 1411 (the 11th year of King Taejong' s reign). King Taejong's concubines Shin and Kwon became *Bhikkhunīs* after King Taejong died and also stayed at Jeongeup-won Temple. Prince Gwang-pyeong, the fifth of eight sons by Queen Sohyun (King Sejong' s wife, r. 1418-1450), died at the age of 20, and his wife, Mrs. Shin, also became a *Bhikkhunī*. His son Youngsoon also died early at 27, and his wife also became a *Bhikkhunī* as her mother-in law did.

The small Jeongup-won Temple (now located in Suseo-dong, Gangnam-gu, Seoul), which was located near Gwangpyeong's tomb, was used as a shrine where large prayer assemblies were held. Bongeun-sa Temple, formerly Gyeonseong-am Hermitage, was established by Queen Yun, royal noble consort of King Seongjong (成宗), and is still a well-known temple in Seoul's Gang-nam district today.

In 1456 (the second year of the reign of King Sejo), after the failure of efforts to restore King Danjeong to power, he and his wife died in exile. King Danjeong's elder sister's husband, Jeong-jong (鄭悰, ?~1461), also died in exile. Afterward, King Danjeong's wife, Queen Jeongsoon and Jeong-jong's wife, Princess Gyunghye, also became *Bhikkhunīs*. In 1463 (the 9th year of King Sejo's reign) Haemin was abbess of Jeongup-won Temple, and Mrs. Yoon, wife of Yoo Ja-hwan (柳子煥, ?~1467), later became its abbess.

After Mrs. Yoon became abbess of Jeongup-won Temple, other royal family woman such as Hyeseon (惠善), Hyemyung (惠明), Hakhye (學惠), Sunhgye (性戒) and Gyeyoon (戒允) all followed her into the order. King Yeonsan-gun's concubine (r. 1494-1506), surname Kwak, became abbess of Jeongup-won Temple in 1522 and spent the rest of her life there praying for the eternal good fortune of the late King Yeonsan-gun. At that time, Wonil (元一) and Myosim (妙心) also entered Jeongup-won Temple. Concubine Kwak was the last abbess of Jeongup-won Temple, according to *Annals of the Joseon Dynasty.*

As seen here, in the latter Joseon Dynasty, the names of many *Bhikkhunīs* appear in inscriptions about eminent Buddhist monks, either in the histories of inscriptions history or in records describing the rebuilding of the temples where they lived. Although *Bhikkhunīs* had a hard life in Korea's mountain temples, there was a continuing increase in the number of *Bhikkhunīs* who tried to uphold and spread Buddhism during the Joseon Dynasty. This was a prelude to the emergence of eminent *Bhikkhunīs* in the modern era. They were pioneers in attracting *Bhikkhunī* disciples and re-establishing *Bhikkhunī Dhamma* Families.

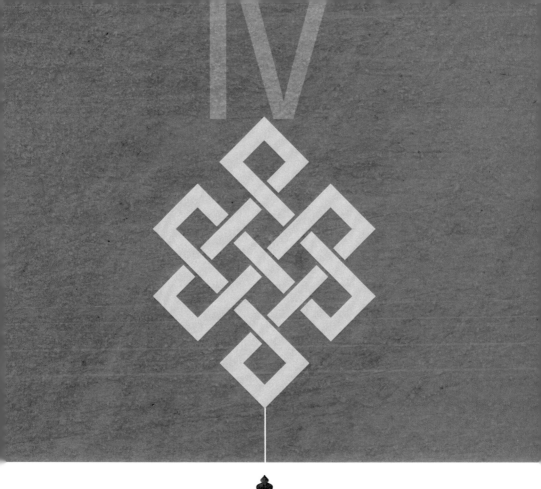

IV

4

The Activities of *Bhikkhunīs* in Korea Today

Mt. Gyeryong-san's Donghak-sa Temple

"The reign of the Buddhist monk in the mountains of the Joseon Dynasty starts at the end of the reign of King Yeonsan-gun (r. 1494-1506), and the oppression of Buddhism was enforced as an irretrievable reality through the anti-Buddhism policy of King Jungjong (r. 1506-1544). In the reign of King Jungjong, where Neo-Confucian influence in politics was so powerful, it was more thorough and perfect than the anti-Buddhism policy of King Yeonsan-gun. If King Yeonsan's anti-Buddhism policy was an unprincipled version of 'disparaging the buddha', the character of King Jungjong's oppression was 'the complete abolition of Buddhism'."

– Lee Bong-choon, *A Study of Buddhist History of Joseon Buddhismp.*484

The above content depicts the grim reality of Joseon Buddhism. Of course, there were times when royal authority

Mt. Hogeo-san's Unmun-sa Temple

Mt. Bulryeung-san's Cheongam-sa Temple

Mt. Gwanggyo-san's Bongnyung-sa Temple

IV. The Activities of *Bhikkhunīs* in Korea Today

encouraged Buddhism, and it reappeared. Buddhism seemed to flourish briefly during the reigns of Kings Sejo and Myeongjong. It all hinged on how much support they had in government or from the throne. But fundamentally, the official government policy of Joseon was to promote Confucianism and reject Buddhism.

If we look at *Bhikkhunīs* today, they are just as dynamic as our busy modern world. That is because the flow of *Dhamma* through the centuries since Buddhism arrived in Korea is becoming more active and apparent. This is partly due to the historical awareness and self-consciousness of *Bhikkhunīs* themselves. They have finally established a worldwide network of contacts and have opened many professional meditation centers. In addition, through their education system, they have made unprecedented achievements in the transmission of doctrinal lineage and precepts.

The inner life of the *Bhikkhunī* order sets the example for self-fulfillment and self-realization and is embodied at Unmun-sa Temple, the biggest *Bhikkhunī* training center in Korea, Mt. Gyeryong-san Donghak-sa Temple, Mt. Bulyoung-san Cheongam-sa Temple, and Mt. Gwanggyo-san Bongnyung-sa Temple. So we can find there the Sutta school

(講院 monk's academy; *Saṅgha* University) and Precept Academy where newly ordained novice monks study the teachings of the Buddha systematically, with a special emphasis on the basic texts of Korean Buddhism. In addition, there are 30 or 40 *Bhikkhunī* Seon Centers to enhance the inner life of *Bhikkhunī*s that are located at temples and hermitages like Mt. Deoksoong-san Gyunsung-am Hermitage, Mt. Sabul-san Yunpil-am Hermitage, Mt. Odae-san Jijang-am Hermitage, Mt. Gaji-san Seoknam-sa Temple and Mt. Cheonseong-san Naewon-sa Temple. The educational level of *Bhikkhunī*s is higher than that of male monks. Since 1990, more than one third of *sāmaṇerī* (novice female monk) have been graduated from elementary college. This proves the basic qualities of *Bhikkhunī*'s temple administration and social role. This reality of the *Bhikkhunī Saṅgha* is a very meaningful phenomenon that gives a certain appropriateness to the change of the present stereotypical structure which is still in the blind spot in the field of our society. We need to shed more light on sexual equality for the future Buddhism.

The life of a *Bhikkhunī* is based on three general aspects of Buddhist practice (三學) required to become a renunciant:

(1) *sīla* (戒/戒學); learning through moral discipline to to guard against the evil consequences of error by word,

deed, or thought;

(2) *samādhi* (定/定學) meditative concentration;

(3) *paññā* (慧) wisdom—the study of Buddhist doctrine
    along with various social activities to benefit society such
    as missionary work, welfare work, cultural activities,
    and Buddhist organization.

Generally speaking, the present form of the *Bhikkhunī* Order
can be classified and explained in the following eight
perspectives:

First is the relationship between teacher and disciple, which
can be compared to the relationship between parent and child.
Members who have been involved are referred to as fellow
students.

Second is *Dhamma* linage (講脈), which describes the
genealogy of the *Dhamma*. *Dhamma* lineages are the 'family
trees' of the Buddhist tradition. *Dhamma* lineages usually
begin with Sakyamuni Buddha and extend down through
various lines (lineages) of Buddhist masters up to the present.
This refers to Buddha's teachings, which is the basis of
wisdom, and the flow of Buddhist teachings, in which one
learns *Dhamma*. It means Sutta education, which was

conducted among the three education (meditation, Buddhist lecture, and chanting) system established during the Buddhist era in the late Joseon Period, and is now called the *Saṅgha* (The Buddhist order or community College).

The third is the flow of the precept linage which seeks to guarantee the purity of the *Bhikkhunī* order by passing on the Buddha's precepts to the teacher then to the student, etc. It encourages temperance and a moral life.

The fourth is the flow of Seon (Zen/ Chan). This is a form of meditation practice that gives us insight in the journey to enlightenment. It is the foundation of the law that *Bhikkhus* of the Korean Buddhist Jogye Order. However, the *Bhikkhunī*s passion for organization in terms of Seon meditation is no less than that of *Bhikkhus*.

The fifth is missionary work. The greatest act of love is to convey the teachings of the Buddha to many people. The word '*Dhamma*' is originally derived from the Indic root *dhr* and has the meaning of 'that which preserves or maintains,' especially that which preserves or maintains human activity. The term has a wide range of meanings in Buddhism, but the foremost meaning is that the teachings of the Buddha are fully in accord with reality, and thus in accord with truth, the true principle and universal law. Its purpose is not to convey faith in salvation, but to see the truth of the universe, the law of being, so that it can be put into practice. It is to bestow all people with wisdom and compassion.

The sixth is welfare work, the practice of compassion, the first of the ten *bodhisatta* practices to cultivate the good qualities (攝善法) outlined in *Fanwangjing pusa jieben shu* (梵網經菩薩戒本疏). The highest form of worship and the highest offering is the giving of self, is to not turn away from anyone in need. This is the most noble teaching that any religion can give to the world and the most compelling command.

The seventh is the field of culture. Culture affects the way people live, and Korea's Buddhist history strongly affects our culture.

The eighth is the organization field. People are said to be social animals. It means that you can not live alone even in religious society. The organization in Buddhism is very important. It is premised on the idea of working together and living together.

1.
Relationship between
a teacher and a disciple (恩上佐緣):

A Respected Teacher is
a Fellow Practitioner

"Soṇa, as you were meditating in private did not a reasoning arise in your mind like this: 'Those who are the Lord's disciplines dwell putting forth energy : I am one of these, yet my mind is not freed from the cankers with no grasping, and moreover there are my family's possessions. It might be possible to enjoy the possessions and to do good. Suppose that I, having returned to the low life, should enjoy the possessions and should do good?'"

"Yes, Lord."

"What do you think about this, Soṇa? Were you clever at the lute's stringed music when formerly you were a householder?"

"Yes, Lord."

"What do you think about this, Soṇa? When the strings of your lute were too taut, was your lute at that time tuneful and fit for playing?"

"No, indeed, Lord."

"What do you think about this, Soṇa? When the strings of your lute were too slack, was your lute at that time tuneful and fit for playing?"

"No, indeed, Lord."

Samhyun *Dhamma* family's Ven. Beophee (right) and Ven. Suock (left) who reconstructed the family's lineage based on memories of past *Dhamma* teachers

Gyemin's 11th *Dhamma* descendent, Ven. Seongmoon (left), who opened the Banya Seon Center at Haein-sa's Samseon-am Hermitage (1926)

Ven. Sooin (front) of the Boun *Dhamma* family and her disciples, Ven. Changbeop, Sungwoo, Youngock, and Hyeyeop (second row from right to left, 1961)

The Cheonghae *Dhamma* family's Ven. Hyechoon and his disciples- Ven. Seoyong (right) and Ven. Jeongan (1979)

Ven. Seongyung of the Yukhwa *Dhamma* family was famous for her high level of practice especially among foreign practitioners. Many foreign practitioners wanted to be her students.

Ven. Ilyeop of the Ilyeop *Dhamma* family and her disciples: Vens.Doseon, Ilyeop, and Gyunghee (left to right, 1970)

> "What do you think about this, Soṇa? When the strings of your lute were neither too taut nor too slack, but were keyed to an even pitch, was your lute at that time tuneful and fit for playing?"
> "Yes, Lord."

-Mahāvagga V : 1

What we study is what we learn, and the most desirable of these is wisdom. Wisdom nourishes confidence and strength of devotion so that the passion for study does not grow weak. The same is true of Buddhist practice, which is based on wisdom. When faith and confidence are weak, people give up.

The son of a rich merchant named Sona Kolivisa was born at the time of Buddha's death. One day, at the invitation of King Bimbisara, he went to 'Eagle Mountain', a narrow, high

The Beopgi *Dhamma* family's Ven. Do-joon (left), Master Ven. Bosung and Ven. Hyeju (1971)

mountain located near Rājagṛha (王舍城) in the ancient Indian state of Magadha. After studying the Buddha's teachings, he become a Buddhist monk. He devoted himself fiercely to the practice of Sitavana near the cemetery outside the royal palace. However, he still could not escape his agonies and obsessions. Even after many years of practice, he was unable to sever his attachments to the world and was worried he would not be able to attain perfect liberation. So he thought it would be better to go back home, enjoy his wealth and do good deeds.

The Buddha heard this and came to see Sona. He then taught him how to practice Buddhism in a way that avoids the extremes of asceticism and self-satisfaction. The content of that conversation is 'the parable of the musical instrument' that appears in *Vinaya piṭaka* (*Mahāvagga* v:1), quoted immediately above.

The Buddha told Sona that if he devoted too much study to this parable, his body and mind would become excited, and if not enough, he would become lazy. We must always maintain balance when we devote ourselves to this parable, and we have to pay attention to our senses so we do not lose our balance and always look back and stay out of the harmony of balance.

Sona, as instructed by the Buddha, finally devoted himself to eliminating the three false views (見結): the false view of a permanent self; the false view of discipline (戒取結); the false view of doubt (疑結). He also vowed to eliminate the three poisons (三毒心) from which all other afflictions arise:

(1) desire, craving (*rāga*);

(2) anger, aversion (*dosa*); and

(3) nescience, folly (*moha*). Sona finally attained enlightenment (阿羅漢), which is absent of all adversity and attachment.

Sona's story emphasizes the importance of a teacher. It

illustrates that a teacher who studies and who is able to hold and check the wavering mind of his student is essential to a practitioner. Sona learned the principles of the middle way of practice and the middle way of life through the Buddha and was finally able to achieve enlightenment. The Buddha often addressed his disciples as "Dear friend!" The lesson of Sona's story is that a master teacher is necessary in one's journey to enlightenment.

This is the relationship between a teacher and a disciple. An ordination teacher permits shaving of renunciant and accepts as a student. A student is a disciple. That is why the relationship between master and disciple can be characterized as the one between parents and child.

Therefore, the most basic relationship in establishing *Dhamma* lineage is the one between teacher and student. Through this relationship, a lineage is formed, and its members gather together to form a close group of fellow practitioners of the same school or master. This also led to the birth of the *Bhikkhunī* Order. There are other names for similar relationships depending on a student's specific relationship with his/her master: precepts disciple, *Dhamma* disciple, *Dhamma* heir, etc.

However, in a Buddhist order, these relationships or ties have another important dimension; that is the pursuit of the common good for individuals, the order and society in general. This also includes the original role of the *saṅgha* (僧伽) which can also be interpreted as 'a group of good friends'. The Buddha often used the term 'friend' when referring to his disciples. The inference is that he himself is not a divine being but one of them. They call it truly from the bottom of heart that goes hand in hand to walk the path of learning and practice of truth (*Dhamma*).

The Buddha said that in order to attain *Nibbāna*, the three poisons from which all other afflictions arise must be eliminated: (1) desire, craving (*rāga*); (2) anger, aversion (*dosa*); and (3) nescience, folly (*moha*). The three poisons previously mentioned can be expunged by practicing the Noble Eight fold Path. It is far more than just a code of conduct. It is the right path and the Buddhist guide to self-enlightenment. This path was taught by Sakyamuni in his first sermon and is one of the cornerstones of Buddhist practice. To follow this path and attain enlightenment one must adhere to the 'eight practices.'

Then one will also be able to lead others to liberation.

The Buddhist scriptures speak much about 'good friends' (*kalyāṇamitta*). Comparatively speaking, in the morning when the sun comes up, there is a forerunner in the way that the east sky first glows first, then the glowing light emanates, and as we rise up the eight sacred paths. In other words, if you have a good friend, you can expect to learn about the eight sacred paths. Sometimes Korean Buddhist minks also refer to each other as '*doban*' (道伴) which can be interpreted as 'companion on the path.'

2.
Buddhist Lecture (講學):
Dhamma is Wisdom

Dhamma is wisdom.

IV. **The Activities of *Bhikkhunīs* in Korea Today**

Donghak-sa Temple's *Saṅgha* College

"Magnificent, venerable sir! Magnificent, venerable sir!
The *Dhamma* has been made clear in many ways by blessed
One, as though he were turning upright what had been turned
upside down, revealing what was hidden, showing the way to
one who was lost, or holding up a lamp in the dark for those
with eyesight to see forms. I go for refuge to the Blessed
One, and to the *Dhamma*, and to the *Bhikkhu Saṅgha*. May I
receive the going forth under the Blessed One, venerable sir,
may I receive the higher ordination?"

-Saṃyutta Nikāya 42:6

This is the way people who have heard the teachings of the
Buddha and confessed their feelings to the Buddha. This verse
seems to have been typified by a single stereotype, since it is
almost always of the same type, as it is seen throughout the

early scriptures. When we enter Buddhism, the first thing we have keep and recite is the Three Refuges (三歸依). This may be the prototype of the Three Refuges.

As you can see, this is the confession of the Buddhist believer who were impressed by the people who heard the Buddha's *Dhamma*. The Three objects (or treasures of veneration 三寶: (1) the Buddha 佛; (2) the *Dhamma* (Buddhist teachings, 法), and (3) the *Saṅgha* (community of order, 僧伽)

If you look at the meaning of it, first it says that 'as if it has caused a fall', it corrects the reversed idea as if you know forever that it changes constantly. As we have shown up to cover, when we take away Tom, Gin, and Thyme, and treat the object with a pure heart, it is as if *Dhamma*, like the fact that we can see the truth of all being as it is, Is the admiration of such a teaching. The *Dhamma*, as 'the wandering man tells the way to him,' realizes the moderate rationality that left both extremes of pleasure and perversion, and 'as if to bring a lamp in the darkness and see the one with the eyes' It is a confession that it guides the folly of wisdom such as mysticism or old consciousness to be a bright wise man.

Those who have met the teachings of the Buddha have been so impressed, and how can they not refute the Buddha and its teachings by such a soul? They became Buddha's disciples on that path, and Buddhism reverted to Buddhism. But their praise for the Buddha did not stop here. It is a confession that expresses the basic nature of the Buddha's teachings, *Dhamma*:

> "He possesses confirmed confidence in the *Dhamma* thus; The *Dhamma* is well expounded by the Blessed One, directly visible, immediate, inviting one to come and see, applicable, to be personally experienced by wise."

- Saṃyutta Nikāya 55:1

This is also a typed phrase identified in many early scriptures. It can be seen that five features of *Dhamma* are presented.

First, 'being realistically probed' means to be realistic because it is based on reality. The belief in God, heaven, past life, endogenous life, postmortem world, etc., is nothing but the belief in 'seeing and believing' or 'being absurd'. That is why the Buddha's teachings are realistic and the Buddha is defined as a realist.

The second Buddha's teachings refer to the time of manifestation, the outcome or action, which means immediate or contemporary teaching, not the same teaching as heaven or the afterlife, which is possible after death.

Third, 'come and see what I can do' refers to open truth and open teachings. The class of Buddhist masters of the majority of practicing religions in India tended to secretly teach the disciples the secret of enlightenment. However, the Buddha proclaimed that there was no secret to proclaim the *Dhamma* because he had spoken to all people without end. It is that the so-called 'do not think that the teaching of the Buddha is hidden in the master's fist'. It was the Buddha's idea that any true successor of illegal (Buddhist law) was a practitioner who learned and practiced self in his fist of *Dhamma*.

The fourth, "to lead to the *Nibbana*", means that the *Dhamma* leads people to the ultimate goal of Buddhism, liberation and nirvana. *Dhamma* is the way we improve our lives.

The fifth, 'The wise man can know for himself', is that Buddha's teaching is the nature of self-awareness that every wise person can know for himself. It is the problem of defilement in my mind, or the trilogy of truth, which means that the structures of *Dhamma* like acting Jenny's smoke all belong to the path of typical consciousness.

That is the Buddha's teaching, *Dhamma*. This can not be expected to be the mysticism, the afterlife, the relief or the salvation that religions are often aiming at. So the Buddha's disciples turned to the Buddha and became disciples of the Buddha after seeing the law of the Buddha, getting the law, knowing the law, realizing the law, solving the doubt, will be. "Follow me." me. That is, a religion that believes in the so-called" "Deity," that is, "to be saved and to have eternal life," and that there is no such thing as teaching or assertion without first understanding, convincing.

This is the most important thing to learn and learn the Buddha's teachings, and that's why I have been concentrating on studying scripture with the focus on Gangwon (*Saṅgha* University) from ancient times. The predicates of lecture, teaching, syllabus, religion, and Buddhism all have their roots in it. There must also be a teacher here, which forms the flow of being the river of today and the school. It is the line of the academic system that can be called the school.

The transmission of Buddhist lecture from *Bhikkhunī* to

Unmun-sa Temple's *Saṅgha* College

Bongnyung-sa Temple's *Saṅgha* College

Cheongam-sa Temple's *Saṅgha* College

IV. **The Activities of** *Bhikkhunīs* **in Korea Today**

Bhikkhunī, which almost coincided with the restoration of independence was started from the three head lecturer of the modern Korean Buddhism, i.e. Ven. Wolgwangdang (月光堂) Geumryong (金龍, 1892~1965), Jungamdang (晶岩堂) Hyeock (慧玉, 1901~1969), and Hwasandang (華山堂) Suock (守玉, 1902~1966).

In the early 1940s, Ven. Suock took over as head lecturer of the Sangju Namjang-sa Temple and opened the Gwaneum Lecture Hall, which was the first of a professional lecture hall. It was supported by the patriarchal teacher Hyebong Bomyung (慧峰普明 1874~1956), who was a patriarchal teacher at the time.

After the restoration of independence, the *Bhikkhunī* professional Sutta schools were established in 1956, starting from Donnghak-sa Temple, established in Cheongdo Unmun-sa Temple, Gimcheon Cheonam-sa Temple, Suwon Bongnyung-sa Temple and others. The representative lecturers succeeding the lecture lineage of the three major head lectures (Ven. Geumryong, Hyeock, and Suock) are Seoul Junggak-sa Temple Ven. Gwangwoo (光雨), Cheongdo Unmun-sa Temple Ven. Myungseong (明星), Suwon Bongnyung-sa Temple Ven. Myoeom (妙嚴), Chunan Yeundae Seon Center Ven.

Jamin (慈珉), the dean of Saṃgha University of Donnghak-sa Temple Ven. Ilchom (一超), the dean of Saṃgha University of Cheongam-sa Temple Ven. Jihyung (志炯), and the dean of Sanseun Saṃgha University Ven. Myoshun (妙洵).

As a professor who have been or are currently working at a college lecture, professor Haeju (海住) is considered one of the best with professor Hyewon (慧諝), Gyehwan (戒環), and Daewon (大原) are currently working at Dongguk University. Bongak (本覺) contributed to the revitalization of the *Bhikkhunī* research by leading the *Bhikkhunī* Research Center of Korea when she was a professor at Joong-ang *Saṅgha* University. In addition, there are Ven. Hyeodo, Ven. Soun (素雲), Ven. Myungbeop (明法), Ven. Seogwang (瑞光), and others now lecturing in the universities.

The fact that the *Bhikkhunī* made *Dhamma*-transmission to the *Bhikkhunī* and the independent lectures of the *Bhikkhunīs*, who were teaching and lecturing *Bhikkhunīs*, were regularized and institutionalized was a major event of the Buddhist sect. These *Bhikkhunīs* who inherited the *Dhamma*-transmission are mostly engaged in the education organizations as lecturers or professors, especially in the specialized Sutta school or the order-supported educational institutions.

Sutta schools

Both *Bhikkhus* and *Bhikkhunī*s have established colleges where the ordained train and study. Only five major sutta schools, with 150 to 250 *Bhikkhunī*s each, exist in Korea, although there are several smaller ones. If a *Bhikkhunī* does not get into one of the main sutta schools, where it is difficult to be accepted, she can go to a smaller sutta school or try to enter a year later, after receiving further training from her teacher. The first year students vary in age from twenty to forty-five. Some nuns may stay for several years with their teacher before going to the sutta school, and some older nuns may bypass the sutta school and go directly to a meditation hall.

Training in the sutta schools is rigorous. The students eat, sleep, and study in one room. Their main teacher lectures about three hours a day, with the *Bhikkhunī*s following the text in Chinese characters, which requires several hours of preparation. Special *Dhamma* lectures are given weekly by visiting teachers, along with various other teachings in the arts, languages, and music. In addition, a work period is scheduled for two or three hours a day, during which the *Bhikkhunīs* look after the vegetable gardens; harvest, pickle, dry, and store food; or cook for the community. The *Bhikkhunīs* in the final year at the sutta schools are in positions of authority and lead the younger nuns. Several will hold yearly, demanding positions such as assistant treasurer, head cook, or office worker. The diet is vegetarian, simple yet nourishing, and often served attractively. Senior *Bhikkhunīs* are offered a slightly different diet, which is less hot and salty, and the sick are given special food as required. Meals are eaten formally, with chanting before and after the meal.

The *Bhikkhunīs* also do work that directly contributes to society, with each nun selecting a yearly project. Some work in orphanages, old people's homes, hospitals, or answer calls on the telephone hotline, while others produce newsletters, and *Dhamma* books, and pamphlets. A few nuns work at Buddhist radio, broadcasting daily Buddhist news, music, chanting, and *Dhamma* talks. Other *Bhikkhunīs* work in Sunday schools and summer retreats for children, or take children from orphanages or the elderly from old peoples' homes on outings. The *Bhikkhunīs* involved in each project raise the funds to do their work.

Although these sutta training schools are considered Buddhist universities in terms of their scholarship, they are more than this. The *Bhikkhunīs* learn to be wholesome, generous people, qualities often lacking in society. They learn not only how to wear their robes, how to eat, and so forth, but also how to communicate with others. In short, they learn how to be satisfied and happy as *Bhikkhunīs*. It is not possible to isolate oneself, for the *Bhikkhunīs* constantly have to interact with each other in community life. Sometimes their interactions are painful, but through these experiences, the nuns know they will become more understanding of others. The nuns go from being very immature people, with lots of fears and unrealistic ideas about monastic life, to becoming more open, accepting, and willing to listen and engage with others. They develop commitment to the community as a whole, and one can see in their faces compassion and wisdom taking shape. Some of these *Bhikkhunīs* become outstanding teachers or leaders.

Sufficient time for meditation is lacking in the sutta schools. The *Bhikkhunīs* attend morning, midday, and evening services in the main Buddha Hall. Doing a variety of communal activities, they learn to be mindful even without long hours of meditation. Hours of chanting and studying the Buddha's teachings helps to calm and deepen the mind; yet I believe more meditation would increase their clarity in daily life. The sutta school I attended had an hour for meditation in the daily schedule, but only a few nuns came. When they are young and busy, they do not appreciate the value of this practice. Nor are they introduced to it properly, although they read a lot about it. Thus, even a graduate from a Buddhist university may not have learned how to meditate well. This is quite unfortunate, yet common. However, a *Bhikkhunī* may do chanting or other practices which purify her mind, and by disciplining herself, she may become a good practitioner.

The *Bhikkhunīs* also have to serve the elder nuns and their teachers. By providing whatever their teachers request or require, the nuns develop a caring attitude toward others. They appreciate this learning situation, which helps them to develop respect and compassion and to diminish arrogance and stubbornness. Upon occasion tempers are short and people abruptly correct each other, but the nuns learn to tolerate such behavior.

IV. **The Activities of *Bhikkhunīs* in Korea Today**

The individuality of the young *Bhikkhunīs* and weakening discipline contribute to this development in recent years. As communities have grown, it is difficult for a few teachers to control large numbers of students. On one occasion some years back, the students demonstrated against the abbess and her staff. This provoked concerns about how sutta schools should be run in order to prevent such situations from getting out of hand. At such times elders from other communities intervene, giving advice and strength.

Korea has one of the most vibrant communities of Buddhist nuns in the world. To my knowledge, only Taiwan has anything even close. While there are still some inequities, such as the tendency for monk's temples to attract more donations, in terms of practice, the nun's community is outstanding.

Two of the major institutions for nuns (and also monks) are the meditation hall (禪房 *seonbang*), and the sutta study program, sutta school (講院 *gangwon*). This is a four-year course of study where one lives at the sutta school with Korean monks, while attending lectures and commentaries. This involves massive amounts of memorization and traditional sino-Korean (Chinese) characters, as well as the daily work you'd expect at a large temple. Only upon completion of one of these courses is a nun (or monk) allowed to take full ordination in Korea. (This applies to only the Jogye Order, although it is by far the largest Buddhist order in Korea.)

Although a number of non-Koreans have ordained in the Jogye Order, few (male or female) have taken full ordination after completing the traditional four-year sutta school course of study. Even now, the number is certainly less than 10 people, although there are several who will graduate in the next year or two. Instead, most foreign *Bhikkhunīs* have ordained through the four-year meditation hall program.

3.
Keeping Precept (持律):
Precept as a teacher

Keeping the precepts with a pure mind

Appropriate regulations are needed to ensure that harmonious unity and activities of *Saṅgha* (Buddhist order or community) are achieved. It is precept. However, the rule of Buddhism differs from that of other religions. For example, if Moses ten precept was a divine revelation in Christianity, then the Buddhist precept was a practical one made according to the situation Buddhist scripture. It is not the organization of the rules from the beginning, but the formation of the unintentional ones by the disciples. So, at that time, according to the circumstances, the article of precept was made timely.

According to the *Vinayapiṭaka*, the 'benefit of enactments (制戒十利)' explains that. On the other hand the *Vinaya of the Four Categories* (四分律) explains that with 'the ten categories of enactments (結戒十句義).' The following is the contents of the *Vinaya of the Four Categories*:

"On account of this, monks, I will make known the course of training for monks, founded on the reasons:

(1) for the excellence of the Order.
(2) for the comfort of the Order.
(3) for the restraint of evil-minded men.
(4) for the ease of well-behave monks.
(5) for the restraint of the cankers belonging to the here and now.
(6) for the combating of the cankers belonging to other worlds.
(7) for the benefit of non-believers.
(8) for the increase in the number of believers.

IV. **The Activities of** *Bhikkhunīs* **in Korea Today**

Bongnyung-sa Temple's Geumgang Vinaya School Dormitory

(9) for establishing *Dhamma* indeed.
(10) for following the rules of restraint."

- *Vinaya of the Four Categories*

On the other hand The contents of the Pali precepts collection is similar as follows:

① For the pirity of the Buddhist order
② For the comfort of the Buddhist order
③ For the control (restrain) of the wicked
④ For the comfortable dwelling of the right renunciants
⑤ For the preventing of all afflictions of this life
⑥ For the prevention of the next life
⑦ For the creating faith of the beings who has no faith
⑧ For the encouragement of faith who already have faith
⑨ For the longer stay in *Dhamma*
⑩ For the precious keeping of the precept

- *Sutta-Vibhaṅga*

This is the benefit of precept. It is basically aiming at cleansing, harmony and comfort of *Saṅgha*, removing the root of suffering, desire and desire, raising the spirit of Buddhist people and Buddhism, and keeping the law for a long time. I can read the reason why the Buddha said, 'Let's make a teacher as a ruler (以戒爲師).'

Keeping precept is to keep the rule like life. In recent years, the reality that the nunnery is based on autonomous mathematical mathematics and produces a scholarship specialist (rhythm) is a high recognition of the nuns' rule. As a result, it is a very encouraging phenomenon that the nuns convey the precept linage to the nuns and form an independent *Dhamma* linage in this field. It refers to the transmission relationship of the so-called *yulsa* (supports of precept). The rise of the nuns (transmission of the teaching from master to disciple) is also established in terms of the rule of precept.

These supports of precepts are the subjects that have been keeping the denomination in line with the teacher of the *Dhamma* lineage who kept the word of the Buddha from the Buddhist practice and wanted to pass on to the posterity. If

The 24th ordination ceremony for female novices (Jogye Order, April 2016)

The 7th Vinaya School graduation ceremony at Cheongam-sa Temple (February 2015)

The 12th Geumgang Vinaya School graduation ceremony at Bongnyung-sa Temple (January 2014)

the system of the jurist is a lenticular lamp, the system of *yulsa* is described as a transgression. It is also the reason why the lawyers who deal with the law are often called the lawer.

The precept study of *Bhikkhunī* is based on the assumption that Jaun Seongwoo (1911 - 1992), a symbol of the *Bhikkhu* preceptor, The precept special-lecture was introduced. In 1951, Myoeom learned about the ordination ritual from the Jaun Seongwoo, and he was appointed as the first preceptor of the order. It led to the commissioning of a committee for the restoration of the full precept *Bhikkhunī* double ordination ritual. As a result, in October 1982, the full precept *Bhikkhunī* double ordination ritual was made in the separate ordination platform of Beomeo-sa Temple, and the tradition of the full precept *Bhikkhunī* double ordination ritual was restored.

To uphold, maintain, or keep something important, especially in the sense of defending or keeping one's faith in the teaching of Buddhism. [Thomas Newhall] After the restoration of the full precept double ordination system of *Bhikkhunī*, a movement that has been visualized in terms of putting the power of self-discipline and practice in the teaching of Buddhism. The good example is the opening of the specialized precept schools such as Suwon Bongnyung-sa Temple Geumgangyulwon (金剛律院 Diamond Precept School) opened by Ven. Myoeom (妙嚴) in June 21, 1999, the Unmun-sa Temple Bohyunyulwon (普賢律院) opened by Ven. Myungseong (明星) in April 4, 2008, and the Cheongam-sa Temple Cheongamyulwon opened by Ven. Jihyung (志炯) in April 18, 2007. It is from this that the transmission of precept lineage of the *Bhikkhunīs* is visualized.

4.
Seon meditation (修禪):
Meditate to Gain Insight

Seon (Zen) meditation is to realize the ultimate truth of the law of dependent origination.

"[One should ask oneself:]

(1) Am I often given to longing or am I without longing?
(2) Am I often given to ill will or am I without ill will?
(3) Am I often overcome by dullness and drowsiness or am I free from dullness and drowsiness?
(4) Am I often restless or am I calm?
(5) Am I often plagued by doubt or am I free from doubt?
(6) Am I often angry or am I without anger?
(7) Is my mind often defiled or is it undefiled?
(8) Is my body often agitated or is it not agitated?
(9) Am I often lazy or am I energetic?
(10) Am I often unfocused or am I focused?"

"If, by such self-examination, a *Bhikkhu* knows he is often given to longing, given to ill will, overcome by dullness and drowsiness, restless, plagued by doubt, angry, defiled in mind, agitated in body, lazy, and unfocused, he should put forth extraordinary desire, effort, zeal, enthusiasm, indefatigability, mindfulness, and clear comprehension to abandon these bad unwholesome qualities, just as one whose clothes are on fire would put forth extraordinary desire, effort, zeal, enthusiasm, indefatigability, mindfulness, and clear comprehension to extinguish it."

- Aṅguttara-Nikāya 10 ⌜*One's Own Mind*⌟ 51

Seon (Chan, Zen) meditation is a practice of meditative concentration that involves fully concentrating the mind on one subject/object without becoming distracted. In a word, it is to unify the mind. The Chinese character is 禪 which is pronounced "Chan" in Chinese, "Zen" in Japanese and "Seon" in Korean. It is derived from the Sanskrit word "*dhyāna*" ("*jhāna*" in Pali). The Chinese character is 定 which means "*samādhi*". *Samādhi* can mean: unification of the mind in concentration; stopping the wandering of the mind and concentrating on one point, subject or object. It is a high level of meditative concentration that requires: mental training through meditation; the skillful unification of mind and object; the mental equanimity conducive to and derived from attention perfectly focused on an object. Literally it means "dwelling in tranquility." Jhana means to be free from attachment to all external things and matters, and *samādhi* means to attain inner peace. It is also called simply "*samādhi*" and is often compared in Mahāyāna with "*paññā*" which means "transcendental wisdom."

The purpose of practicing meditative concentration is to control the mind and acquire wisdom and compassion. Our everyday minds are coarse and undisciplined like the waves on the ocean. To control the mind is to silence and calm these waves. Meditation's goal is to stop the flow of thought. *Samatha* is meditation to achieve serenity. *Samatha* is synonymous with concentration and *samādhi*. Technically, *samatha* is defined as "the one-pointedness of mind or concentration to attain peace of mind." It is a precondition to attaining *samādhi*.

Samatha is part of three supreme principles that are inseparable from Buddhism: 1) Sila or precepts (five precepts, eight precepts, etc.) 2) *Samādhi* or concentration (four and nine stages of meditation, etc.) 3) *Paññā* or transcendental wisdom (the four noble truths, twelve links of dependent arising, etc.)

Samatha helps one attain a calm concentrated mind to give one the insight to see through one's body, mind, and even the world. *Samatha* is *vipassanā* practice. *Samatha* is a method of meditation that causes the object of meditation to be changed, created or vanquished. This is the ultimate enlightenment of the Buddha.

The Buddha taught his disciples to persevere in meditation practice to gain insight. If you are not proficient at knowing another's mind, you should at least know your own. Then how do you become proficient at knowing the workings of your own mind? The Buddha gave this analogy:"When a person tries to beautify themselves using a mirror, if they see a flaw, they try to fix it or cover it up. If they see no imperfections, they think they are fine. To reflect on oneself is helpful to improving one's good qualities."

The path to Mt. Deoksoong-san's Gyunsung-am Hermitage

Ganhwa Seon (看話禪) meditation is the most predominant practice of the Jogye Order of Korean Buddhism. Unlike *Samatha* and *Vipassanā*, Ganhwa seon originated from patriarchal Chan (Seon/Zen) (祖師禪), which was initially transmitted from Bodhidharma (菩提達磨) to the sixth patriarch Huineng. Ganhwa seon is also called hwadu Seon (話頭禪) which is a form of meditation that focuses on a key phrase or word, usually taken from officially recognized Zen dialogues or riddles (*"koan"*).

What is a hwadu (話頭 lit." speech-head" ; key phrase)? "Hwa" (話) is the Chinese character for "speech or spoken phrase "while "du" (頭), means "head" (that which precedes speech). A hwadu is the keyword or phrase that is isolated in one's mind for constant investigation throughout one's waking moments during meditation, which some define as "turning inward to self-illumination with unremitting singularity."

Other translations are: critical phrase, true-word of no-word, sign post, and Cyclopean doubt. It is a word or phrase that demands an immediate answer but which cannot be solved by intellect because the answer does not consist of words.

A hwadu is the source of a word before it is uttered; it is

the inexpressible ultimate truth of what practitioners call a "living phrase." It is a method or device employed in a Seon dialogue between master and student to arouse doubt about the "keyword." This will shut down all possible avenues of rationalization to help us find our "original face" or "true self-nature"; it will unite us with the universe, our Buddha-nature, or our "true-suchness." It is also a kind of nonsensical question to a student for which an immediate answer is demanded, yet one cannot rely on reason. As mentioned above, the first syllable "hwa-" of hwadu 話頭 means phrase, and the second syllable "-du" or "head" is a particle in classical Chinese and has no specific meaning.

This explanation of Ganhwa Seon (看話禪) tells us that we can attain the enlightenment of the Buddha by intuiting the mind without the hindrance of words or teachings. So, traditionally, the following four principles have been regarded as the main doctrines of Seon (Chan/Zen):

1) "Separate transmission outside of the teaching." (教外別傳) This expresses the concept that the transmission of enlightenment occurs by direct interaction between teacher and student or through one's own direct insight

IV. **The Activities of** *Bhikkhunīs* **in Korea Today**

and not through the study of doctrine. This is a Buddhist teaching that is traditionally said to have been introduced into China by Bodhidharma (菩提達磨).

2) "No establishment of words and letters." (不立文字). This slogan came into popular in use in the Chan Buddhism of Song China. It expresses the Chan School's desire to de-emphasize dependence on the tradition of scriptural study. On the basis of personal practice, it indicates the need for the enlightened mind to remain unfettered by linguistic constructs.

3) "Directly pointing to the mind." (直指人心). This refers to the characteristic Chan technique where the teacher directly enlightens the student by showing the student his/her own true mind. This can be done without reliance on verbal teachings.

4) "To see one's own true nature and attain Buddhahood on one's own." (見性成佛). A slogan that encourages practitioners to seek direct experience for themselves, rather than relying on the words and explanations of teachers and scriptures. The implication is that, in

essence, there is no difference between an ordinary person and the Buddha.

Historically, these principles have their roots in three instances in Buddhist scriptures of the direct mind-to-mind transmission of enlightenment (以心傳心). They all took place between the Buddha and his disciple Mahā-Kassapa:

1) At the Buddha's sermon on Vulture Peak when Buddha held up a flower and Mahā-Kassapa acknowledged with a smile.

2) At the Pagoda of Many Children when Buddha shared his seat with Mahā-Kassapa.

3) When the Buddha lifted his foot out of his coffin under the twin sala trees at Kusinārā.

As these principles reveal, Ganhwa Seon is a method that requires a completely different form of intuition than the analytical approach of most Buddhist schools.

The Seon practice of *Bhikkhunīs* is thorough and intensive and worthy of praise. Prominent and well-known *Bhikkhunīs* are well-known and considered models of intensive Seon practice. Today we can observe easily the sincere and fervent Seon practice of *Bhikkhunīs* at the 30~40 Seon meditation halls scattered across the country, including Gyunseong-am Hermitage on Mt. Deoksoong-san (established in 1916.1).

Bhikkhunī Seon centers in Korea were established by *Bhikkhunīs* and is where they go to study meditation. *Bhikkhunī* Seon centers built before Korea's liberation from Japan include: Gyunsung-am Hermitage, Sorim Seon Center on Mt. Naejang-san (established in 1924), Donghwa-sa Temple's Budo-am Seon Center (established in 1928), Yoonpil-am Hermitage's Sabul Seon Center (established in 1931), and Jigang-am Hermitage's Seon Center on Mt. Odae-san. They are all still operating.

Today, about 800 to 1,000 *Bhikkhunīs* attend the 3-month biannual meditation retreats every year. In comparison, about 1,200 to 1,400 *Bhikkhus* attend them at 60 meditation centers around Korea, so the difference in numbers is not that great. The opening of *Bhikkhunī* Seon centers and their growing participation in these retreats bode well for the future of Korean *Bhikkhunīs*.

During meditation seasons, the discipline in the meditation halls is very strong. As in all Korean temples, those in the

Sabul-jeon Hall is a symbol of Mt. Sabul-san's Yoonpil-am Hermitage. Rocks resembling buddhas are seen on four sides of the hall.

Girin Seon Center at Mt. Odae-san's Jijang-am Hermitage. Ven. Bongong of the Bongrae *Dhamma* Family opened this Seon (Zen) Center.

IV. **The Activities of *Bhikkhunīs* in Korea Today**

Chunchuk Seon Center at Bulyoung-sa Temple

Baekheung-am Seon Center, the filming site for 'On the Road'.

Mt. Palgong-san's Budo-am Seon Center. Ven. Seongmoon of the Gyemin *Dhamma* Family opened it in 1928.

Geumdang Seon Center at Gamsan-sa Temple in Gyeongju's historic district

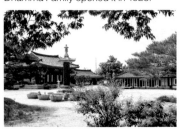

Chungyungrim Seon Center at Heungryun-sa Temple, a well-known *Bhikkhunī* Seon Center in Gyeongju.

meditation halls get up very early, usually about 2:00 or 3:00 A.M. Until they go to bed, which may be 10:00 or 11:00 P.M., they have minimal personal time. They meditate for ten to fourteen hours a day and the atmosphere is light and joyous.

After finishing sutta school, a nun may choose life in the meditation hall. About a quarter of those attending sutta school go on to become meditation nuns after they graduate. Most nuns choose to live in a small temple with their teacher, become abbess in their own temples, or take graduate courses at a major Buddhist university. A few choose social work or other professional areas but these too need further studies at a university.

In Korea, there are at least ten large meditation halls, each having fifty to one hundred nuns, and about fifteen medium meditation halls having ten to thirty nuns. There are also many small gatherings with just a few nuns meditating together. Often located in beautiful areas, the meditation halls may be part of a large nuns' temple or near a large monks' temple. If so, the hall is in a quiet area away from visitors and tourists.

There are two major meditation seasons—in the summer

and the winter—each lasting three months, and in the spring and autumn there are two-month "off-season" retreats. Most large meditation halls are open year round and the most serious practitioners stay and practice continuously there. In some temples, nuns undertake retreats for three years or more and are not allowed to leave the temple under any circumstances during that time, unless they are very sick.

In the meditation hall nuns alternate sitting for fifty minutes and walking for ten minutes, with three-hour sessions before dawn, in the morning, afternoon, and evening. The basic discipline of the meditation hall is decided at a meeting at the beginning of the retreat. At this time, the meditation hall nuns also choose who will be the leader of the hall and assign other work positions that keep the temple functioning well. In the past *Bhikkhunīs* had to cook and heat the rooms by making fires, but now electricity and modern conveniences have taken over these difficult chores in many temples.

The *Bhikkhunīs* sit in order of seniority, according to the number of years they have been ordained. The head of the meditation hall is in charge of training the younger nuns. If a younger *Bhikkhunī* has a problem with her meditation, she goes to this nun, who either helps her or takes her to see a master. Almost all the meditation halls are affiliated with a main temple where there is a master. At the beginning of the meditation season, and once every two weeks, the nuns attend a talk by this master or listen to a taped talk if they are unable to go. If the main temple is far away, they hear a *Dhamma* talk only a few times during the meditation season, and the elder *Bhikkhunīs* take over the responsibility of guiding the younger nuns in the meantime.

The day before a lecture, the *Bhikkhunīs* bathe and look after their personal needs. They do whatever chores need to be done and sometimes relax or go for a walk in the mountains. After listening to the *Dhamma* talk the following day, they continue with the meditation schedule. The days go by very quickly, and one finds that four or five hours of sleep is sufficient. If drowsiness occurs in meditation, one corrects her posture and continues to practice diligently. Along with meditation practice, some nuns may chant or bow as repentance practice during break times. They often do some exercise, *T'ai Chi* or yoga, but generally this is not a communal function.

The cushions in the hall are laid out very close to one

another, with the nuns facing the wall when meditating. They do a *koan* practice. Here a *Bhikkhunī* receives a *koan* from a master and works with it throughout her life. This differs from Japanese Zen, where one goes through a series of *koans* which open to many aspects of the one. In Korea they work with the one which will open to many aspects of the others. A nun's mind should not become attached to the words or the storyline of the *koan*.

In this way, she comes to the essence. Some teachers give the *koan*, "What is it?" or "What is this?" In other words, "What is this mind? What is this thing we call I or me?" A story accompanies each *koan*, and hopefully one is left with a puzzle or a deeper sense of doubt about this question. If practice is very strong, one goes beyond the words and is left with a very curious, open, aware sense of inquiry from moment to moment. If inquiry into the *koan* is not alive, one often finds that one is dreaming, deluded, or lethargic.

A person who is not interested in diligent practice will not last very long in the meditation halls, but one who has practiced a long time has this very "alive word." The question becomes a doubt or sensation of curious unknowing, and one is completely absorbed in this present moment. Serious practitioners have a certain joy and strength that pervades them, and others' problems seem to dissolve in their presence. At the least, these practitioners show us how to work with and resolve problems.

Some practitioners in Korea now do other practices: *vipassana* they learned from Southeast Asian monks or Tantra learned from Tibetans. From my observation, providing that one does not disturb others or expect them to follow, it is acceptable to engage in other practices. Such practitioners are usually quiet about their practice.

There is a certain uniformity and consistency among the *Bhikkhunīs* in the meditation hall. Of course the *Bhikkhunīs* are individuals, but they perform their duties quietly and contentedly without drawing attention to themselves. The junior nuns are quickly reprimanded if they stand out and are taught how to live amicably within the hall. If a nun is sick, she may go to the infirmary, and if her posture is painful, she can change her position. But because one sits for long periods, movement within the meditation session naturally becomes less and less.

The hall has a sense of lightness, humor, and joy. Each day the *Bhikkhunīs* share tea and talk together. The senior nuns talk about the masters and great nuns they knew, thus informally giving teachings and guidance on how to practice. Having tea together is an important part of the practice, and young *Bhikkhunīs* who do not want to attend are reprimanded. Unless one is old or sick, she is expected to share in all activities, even social times.

Once a season a week of non-sleep practice occurs. During this week every effort is exerted to sit upright and concentrate on one's *koan*. A long thin stick is gently tapped on the shoulders of a dozing nun with a cracking sound that alerts the whole room. The days and nights pass, but not without great effort and suffering to stay alert. However, as thoughts and dreams diminish, the mind becomes clear and lucid. On the last morning, the nuns trek in the mountains to get some exercise before resting.

At the end of the season, the nuns are free to continue sitting in the meditation hall or they may travel to other meditation temples. Although the atmosphere may differ depending on whether a hall is close to the city or in magnificent mountain scenery, the meditation halls are generally run in the same way, so the nuns have little difficulty going from one to another.

Close relationships are not encouraged within nuns' communities, and if two nuns are seen together for a long period of time, they are encouraged to separate and will not be accepted in a meditation hall at the same time. Financial support of the meditation *Bhikkhunīs* is minimal. They receive food and lodging for the three months and a small amount of money when they leave to cover their fare to another temple. Unlike the monks, they are not well supported financially, and very few of the meditation *Bhikkhunīs* have much money. Their clothes are often old and patched, and they have few possessions. All of the *Bhikkhunīs* support each other well, giving freely if they have something that someone else needs.

Not all *Bhikkhunīs* enter a meditation hall after completing sutta school. Some enter a graduate program in Buddhist studies or social work at a university. A few *Bhikkhunīs* study secular subjects to become doctors, lawyers, artists, or performers. Others are involved in the Buddhist radio and television, which have become very popular recently. One

IV. **The Activities of *Bhikkhunīs* in Korea Today**

nun has become a famous radio announcer with a popular rating and raises funds for social projects in the community.

The working monastics usually live alone or with one other monastic and are not very adept in communal life. Few have ever lived in meditation halls, although many have completed sutta study schools. However, because they have missed out on the nuns' communal life, their monastic quality is lacking.

A *Bhikkhunī* is sometimes expected to hold a position in a temple: abbess, administrator, secretary, director, treasurer, or head of the kitchen. Usually *Bhikkhunīs* are persuaded to take on these difficult positions due to their seniority, abilities, or popularity. Rarely do they choose to be an administration monastic, as it requires time and effort in areas that are not so conducive to practice and peace of mind. Of course, a mature person will use this opportunity to strengthen and deepen her path. On completion of her duty, she happily returns to the meditation hall or to her home temple to continue her practice.

Elderly *Bhikkhunīs* are also represented in the *Bhikkhunī* Order. To strengthen the status of *Bhikkhunīs*, the National *Bhikkhunī* Association of Korea's Jogye Order held its 9th meeting on March 24, 2016 and for the first time scheduled

29 conferences to deal with elderly *Bhikkhunī* issues. At the meeting, honorary members of the Council of Elders included: Vens. Gyeongsoon, Hyehae, Gwangwoo, Jingwan, Beopun, Gyeonghee, Jeongrun, Gyeongsim, Sungta, Hyunmook, and Beopyong. Full members of the Council included: Vens. Myungseong, Jaehee, Myogwan, Bogak, Hyeun, Jagwang, Undal, Soohyun, Beophee, Bulpil, Jahaeng, Jaeun, Jamin, Hyejoon, Myungsoo, Haengdon, and Ilbeop. They are all *Bhikkhunīs* who have left their mark in this field.

Especially the late patriarch, deceased member of the Korean Seon/Zen lineage; usually those whose *Dhamma* descendants (heirs in subsequent generations) are still flourishing at present. They had kept the sole great purpose for the Buddha's appearance in this world (一大事因緣), the most important cause, viz., to become enlightened and save all sentient beings from sufferings.

Their names are as follows: Ven. Beophee (法喜, 1887~1975)· Seongmoon (性文, 1895~1974)· Manseong (萬性, 1897~1975)· Wolhye (月慧, 1895~1956)· Ilyeop (一葉, 1896~1971)· Sooin (守仁, 1899~1997)· Junghaeng (淨行, 1902~2000)· Bongong (本空, 1907~1965)· Jinoh (眞悟, 1904~1994)· Seongyung (禪敬, 1904~1996)·

Daeyoung (大英, 1903~1985)· Inhong (仁弘, 1908~1997)· Hyechoon (慧春, 1919~1998)· Jangil (長一, 1916~1997)· Beopil (法一, 1904~1991)· Geungtan (亘坦, 1885~1980)· Eunyoung (恩榮, 1910~1981)· Jahyun (慈賢, 1896~1988)· Injeong (仁貞, 1899~1978)· Yoonho (輪浩, 1907~1996)· Dojoon (道準, 1900~1992)· Queyoo (快愈, 1907~1974)· Cheonil (天日, 1912~1977)· Jimyung (智明, 1921~2013)· Kwangho (光毫, 1915~1989)· Myungsoo (明洙, 1925~2013)· Dowon (道圓, 1904~1971)· Myungjoo (明珠, 1904~1986)· Iljo (日照, 1910~1990)· Eungmin (應敏, 1923~1984)· Sedeung (世燈, 1926~1993)· Sangryun (相侖, 1929~2007), and others.

5.
Missionary Activities (布教):

To Spread *Dhamma* (Teachings) is the Greatest Act of Compassion

Even though you travel to countless worlds
And even though you read and carry countless suttas,
If you cannot save sentient beings
You cannot say you have repaid the Buddha's grace.

- Mahāprajñāpāramitā-śāstra

Spreading the *Dhamma* (the Buddha's teachings) is a demanding call in today's Buddhism. It is also a way to repay the Buddha's grace. Nothing is more important or urgent than transmitting the *Dhamma* to the public and leading a life of happiness.

The year after the Buddha attained enlightenment, five

Foreigners' Lotus Lantern Festival
on Buddha's Birthday

young *Bhikkhus*, Koṅḍañña, a man named Yasa and four of his friends, and 50 others attained the state of *arahant* (the highest level of sainthood in Hīnayāna). The Buddha then urged them to go forth and teach.

Then the Lord addressed the monks, saying:

> "I am freed from all snares, both those of devas and those of men. And you too are freed from all snares, both those of devas and those of men. Go forth and teach for the blessings of the many and for the happiness of the many. Do this out of compassion for the world, for the welfare, the blessing, the happiness of devas and men. Do not travel together; each must take a separate path. Teach the *Dhamma* which is lovely at the beginning, lovely in the middle, and lovely at

the end. There are people with dust in their eyes, who, not knowing the *Dhamma*, are decaying. But if they learn the *Dhamma*, they will grow. And I, monks, will go to Uruvelā, to the camp township, in order to teach the *Dhamma*."

-Saṃyuttâgama-sūtra (Agama of Combined Discourses) 39, 1096 繩索縛

That is what the Buddha is telling us. His teachings are not the only absolute truth, and we should follow him. The Buddha's teaching is not a fiction that we will have eternal life and be reborn into heaven or paradise. The above passage can also be found in the Pāli scriptures (*Saṃyutta Nikāya* 4:5) and *Vinayapiṭaka* (*Mahāvagga*).

Buddhist missionary work is to spread the *Dhamma* to benefit, comfort and give happiness to all beings. And that is why propagating the *Dhamma* is the greatest act of compassion.

If Puṇṇa Mantāṇiputta said to be the most famous for her eloquence in preaching the *Dhamma* among *Bhikkhus*, the Buddha admired that Dhammadinnā was the most famous for his eloquence in preaching the *Dhamma* among *Bhikkhunīs*. Dhammadinnā was the wife of a Visākhā merchant living in Rajagaha, the capital city of Magadan, and these are the best couple in Buddhist history.

Visākhā was a member of the saints, although he was a lay-person. He listened to the Buddha's sermon three times. When he heard first time, he attained the stage of *stream-enterer* (須陀洹 *sotāpanna*: The practitioner succeeds in breaking the deluded view of the three worlds, and pushing his/her own karmic flow clearly onto the path of enlightenment). When heard twice, he attained the stage of *once-returner* (斯陀含 *sakadāgāmin*: A religious practitioner who will only be reincarnated in this world or in one of the heavens one more time). When heard three times, he attained the stage of *non-returner* (不還果 *anāgāmin* : A practitioner of the path of the *sāvaka* 聲聞 who has fully severed the afflictions of the desire realm). When Dhammadinnā expressed his intention, he was the one who led her renunciation.

Dhammadinnā attained the stage of *Arahant* (阿羅漢: Worthy, venerable; an enlightened, saintly man; the highest type or ideal saint in Hīnayāna) thanks to the active support from her husband. Since then, Dhammadinnā had been praised by many fellow nuns or the public, and every time she says, people praised her preach."It is as easy and clear as cutting a stem of a lotus by a knife."So the Buddha wrote about Dhammadinnā *Dhamma* Dinhna in the sutta, Dhammapada as follows:

"Her I call a brāhmaṇa (arahant), who does not cling to the past,future and present aggregates and who is free from moral defilements and attachment."

- Dhammapada 421

How was the practical propagation of contemporary *Bhikkhunīs*? Their missionary can be roughly classified as the 'sprouting time' of 1960s, the 'spreading period' of 1970s, and 'practical period' of 1980s.

The leader of popular missionary was the propagation for the children. In the 1960s, Ven. Chun-il (天日) of Seokbul-sa Temple at Mapo-gu in Seoul and Ven. Gwang-woo (光雨) of Jeonggak-sa Temple at the Samseon-dong in Seoul opened the children's *Dhamma* meeting for the first time. In 1965, Ven. Chun-il, together with the Buddhist nun Unmun (雲門) organized the Mapo Yeonhwa Children's Association at the Seokbul-sa Temple and opened the first children's *Dhamma* meeting. Since then, the Buddhist community has provided facilities for 30 kindergartens and 25 nursery schools as a facility for children's propagation and education, which is an eloquent activity of the *Bhikkhunīs*.

After the opening of the Lumbini kindergarten Gwaneum

Seonwon by Ven. Jihaeng (智行) in Asan, Chungnam province for the first time in 1985. In 1987, Eunyoung kindergarten was opened by the *Bhikkhunī* temple Bomun-sa, Seoul. Here are other children's facilities opened by *Bhikkhunīs*: Naksan Nursery in Seoul (1981); Lumbini Nursery in Asan; Eunyoung Nursery in Seoul (established by Bomun-sa Temple); Anam Nursery (established by Ven. Hyedo); Ocksoo Nursery (established by Ven. Sangduck); Aga Garden in Pyeongtaek (established by Ven. Hwajeong); Borisu Children's Home in Ulsan (established by Ven. Seonho); Cheongsu Children's House in Daegu (established by Ven. Jongyeol); and Seonglim Children's House in Gyeongju (established by Ven. Jimyung).

In the missionary of youth group, the Ven. Sung-il (性一) of Sinheung-sa Temple in Hwasung city is praised for the *bodhisatta's* vow of edification in the youth propagation. He published the Children's Buddhist School Guidebook, Guideline for the Youth Propagation, and the Guideline for the Lay Buddhist Propagation. Since 1973, he built 1,000-pyeong youth training center for the first time in Buddhist circle, and has been providing the guidelines of youth propagation since 1973, educating about 3,000 young people every year.

In the fields of Buddhist counseling and propagation, the

Missionary work, the practice of compassion /
Children's Templestay program

Buddhist Counseling Development Institute was established in April 2000. Prior to its establishment, Ven. Jeongdeok, who served as its second and third chief director, began a phone counseling service called 'Call of Compassion' in March 1990. There are now more than ten professional *Bhikkhunī* counselors working for this counseling service, including its current director Ven. Dohyeon.

In the field of Buddhist ministry to the military, Ven. Myungbeop was assigned by the Special Diocese of the Jogye Order in 2014 became the first *Bhikkhunī* officer in Korean military history. Other *Bhikkhunīs* working in this field are Vens. Hotaek, Backgeo, Deokhyun, Daehae, Seojang, Ji-il, and others.

In the field of ministering to prisoners and police, which began in Daegu's penitentiary in 1960, more than 70 *Bhikkhunīs* have been commissioned as committee members by the Ministry of Justice. Among them are Vens. Jamin, Myungwoo, Sangdeok and Jeonghyun. Some *Bhikkhunīs* also belong to the Police Buddhist Order which was founded in January 1987. Among them are Ven. Seong-il, Jeongmyung, Gyungryun, and Boan.

Some *Bhikkhunīs* doing missionary overseas are: Ven. Gwangok from Bulgwang-sa working in Toronto; Ven. Beopchun from Bulsim-sa working in Chicago, Ven. Wonmyung from Wonmyung-sa working in Los Angeles; Vens. Hyeyoung and Seonmook from Yeonguk-sa, and Vens. Domyung and Myoji from Jogye-sa working in New York City.

Ven. Daehaeng (大行, 1927-2012) of Daehaeng Seon Center in Anyang also sent ten *Bhikkhunīs* abroad as international missionaries: four to the United States, two to Argentina, and one each to Canada, Germany, Thailand and Brazil. There are now about 30 *Bhikkhunīs* active in the International Missionary Association which was founded in 1998.

Korea's 'Templestay Program' is a program that allows the general public and foreigners to broaden their understanding of Buddhism by spreading the spiritual culture of Korea. Their slogan is 'My Journey of Happiness'. Templestay is an experiential program in Korean Buddhism initiated by the Jogye Order of Korean Buddhism at the onset of the 2002 World Cup. During its 1,700 years of history, Korean Buddhism has preserved and passed down Ganhwa Seon practice, a kind of Seon (Zen) meditation. Every year during the Buddhist meditation retreat seasons (three months in summer and three months in winter), about 2,500 monastics enter a 100-day meditation retreat at one of the 100 temples nationwide. This is a unique Korean tradition in the sphere of Mahayana Buddhism.

This tradition has influenced the architectural layout of temples and monastic life over the years, and one can attain inner calm and peace of mind and body at any of these temples. In their effort to transform the 2002 World Cup into a cultural opportunity, the Jogye Order of Korean Buddhism decided to open their temple gates during the games and allowed both Koreans and non-Koreans to stay in one of their mountain temples.

As a result, in the 30 days the World Cup lasted (May 31, 2002 to June 30), 1,000 foreigners and 10,000 Koreans experienced the Templestay program. That was a sizable achievement, but more importantly, Korean Buddhism and the Templestay program became known to the wider world as major international media, including CNN, the New York Times, BBC and NHK, paid growing attention and reported feature stories about them.

After the end of the 2002 World Cup, the Jogye Order of Korean Buddhism announced the permanent establishment of the Templestay program on July 2, 2002. The Order then established the Cultural Corps of Korean Buddhism on July 16, 2004 as an operative body to run the Templestay program. As the national government promised budget support, the number of temples operating a Templestay program grew from 31 in the first year to 110 in 2015.

The Templestay program is now recognized as one of the

major tourist programs in Korea. In 2009, the OECD selected the Templestay program as one of the five most successful combinations of culture and tourism.

The Templestay Program began with 31 pilot temples in 2002, and between 2004 and 2013, 236 more temples applied to participate in the program. As of 2017, 137 temples were operating Templestay programs. *Bhikkhunī* temples that offer this program are: Daewon-sa in Sancheong, Bongnyung-sa in Suwon, Shinheung-sa in Hwaseong, Beopryun-sa in Yongin, Hwaun-sa in Yongin city, and Jingwan-sa in Seoul.

According to the Korean Buddhist Cultural Foundation, Templestay participation increased steadily between 2004 and 2017. As of today, 1,843,271 Koreans and 299,780 foreigners have participated, averaging 131,662 Koreans and 21,413 foreigners a year. Korean participants had a high interest in healing, and foreigners showed a high interest in Korean traditional culture. Such data will be useful in developing future Templestay programs to fulfill the 'missionary' goals of the Jogye Order.

Temples desiring to participate in the program must be approved after submitting an application to the Korean

Buddhist Cultural Foundation. Upon receipt of the prescribed documents, the Foundation's selection committee will evaluate the application and the temple's operational plan and decide whether or not to designate preliminary operations inspectors for an on-site inspection. If approved, the temple will be accepted on a one-year probationary period, and if there are no problems, it will be officially designated a Templestay temple.

6.
Welfare (福祉):
The Ultimate Practice is Giving

One practitioner was suffering from dysentery. He had diarrhea and was lying in filth. The Buddha, accompanied by Ānanda, looked at him and spoke. Their conversation was as follows:

> "What is your disease, monk?"
> "Lord, I have dysentery."
> "Have you no one to attend to you?"
> "I have not Lord."
> "Why don't the other monks attend to you?"
> "I am of no use to them, so they do not attend to me."

> *- Mahāvagga* Ⅷ:26

This scene is described in detail in the sutta *Mahāvagga* Ⅷ:26. During the conversation, the Buddha told Ānanda to bring water. Then he took one sick person and put him on a bed. The Buddha then spoke to another practitioner in the temple and asked him if he was sick, what his illness was, and who was attending to him. And so the Buddha said:

> "Monks, you have no mother and no father to attend to you. If you do not attend to one another, then who will attend to you? Anyone who would tend to me should also tend to the sick."
>
> "If a monk has a preceptor, he should be tended to for life by his preceptor until he recovers. If a monk has a teacher, he should be tended to for life by his teacher until he recovers. If a monk has someone who shares his dwelling... And if he has a pupil... And if he has a fellow-preceptor... And if he has a fellow teacher... If one has neither a preceptor nor a teacher, nor one who shares his dwelling, nor a pupil, nor a fellow-preceptor, nor a fellow-teacher, he should be tended to by the Order. If no one tends to him, it is an offense of wrong-doing."
>
> -*Mahāvagga* VIII:26

Here, we get a glimpse of the Buddha's humanity. The humanitarian aspect of Buddhism is found in many places in early scriptures. It is inevitable that we are born into this world, grow old, grow sick, and die. However, we tend to think these things happen only to others and not us. That is life.

Afterward. the Buddha told his disciples this:

> "Sickness, old age and death are three angels sent to this world. It is fortunate to receive their enlightenment, but he who encounters them and does not attain enlightenment will mourn forever."

The life history is the relationship between needle and thread cannot be separated. That is because they are in a cause and effect relationship, and cause and effect relationships are the source of suffering. Buddha identified 'twelve links of dependent arising' (十二緣起) that control the interrelated relationships in our lives. When inquiring into what it is that gives rise to human suffering, the Buddha found it to be a continuum of twelve phases of conditioning that occur in a regular order.

These twelve links of conditioned existence and the symbols he used to illustrate them are:

(1) nescience/ a blind woman

(2) action/ a potter at work or man gathering fruit

(3) consciousness/ a restless monkey

(4) name and form/ a boat

(5) sensory organs/ a house

(6) contact/ a man and woman sitting together

(7) sensation/ a man pierced by an arrow

(8) desire/ a man drinking wine

(9) craving/ a couple in union

(10) existence/ childbirth

(11) birth/ a man carrying a corpse

(12) disease, old age and death/ an old woman leaning on a
    stick.

In this order, the prior situation is the condition for the arising of the next situation. Also, in the same order, if the prior condition ceases, the next condition ceases. As you can see from the story of the three angels, even the most precious thing that will mature me, we cannot understand the truth. Buddhism's 'three poisons' are wrapped around us, falling into desire and obsession, lazy to look at other beings inter-related to us.

In Buddhism, these poisons are explained in terms of the three basic afflictions from which all other afflictions arise: (1) desire, craving (貪欲 *rāga*); (2) anger, aversion (瞋恚 *dosa*); and (3) nescience, folly (愚癡 *moha*).

This is the lesson of the Buddha. The story of the three angels tells us that it is possible to see the reality of our life as it is symbolized in our daily life. We do not realize that we are in pain or difficulty in this life. By realizing the precious lesson of three angels and wake up my body, mouth, and will to repair bad things and practice good conduct. A life of giving is the Buddhist way of welfare. Giving is a gift; generosity, donation, charity, almsgiving, i. e. of goods, or the doctrine, with resultant benefits now and also hereafter in the forms of reincarnation, as neglect or refusal will produce the opposite consequences.

In Buddhism, it is seen divided into a range of multiple categories: The five kinds are giving to those who have come from a distance, those who are going to a distance, the sick, the hungry, those wise in the doctrine. The seven kinds are giving to visitors, travelers, the sick, their nurses, monasteries, endowments for the sustenance of monks or nuns, and clothing and food according to season. The eight kinds are giving to those who come for aid, giving for fear (of evil), return for kindness received, anticipating gifts in return, continuing the parental example of giving, giving in hope of rebirth in a particular heaven, in hope of an honored name, for the adornment of the heart and life.

Charity is one of the four embracing practices (四攝事) of the *bodhisattas*; it is also one of the six perfections (六波羅蜜) and one of the six kinds of mindfulness.

So the Buddha describes the virtue of giving as follows in the scripture *Saṃyutta Nikāya* (1:41-42):

> "What is given yields pleasant fruit,
> But not so what is not given.
> Thieves take it away, or kings,
> It gets burnt by fire or is lost."

> "Then in the end one leaves the body
> Along with one's possessions.
> Having understood this, the wise person
> Should enjoy himself but also give.
> Having given and enjoyed as fits his means,
> Blameless he goes to the heavenly state."

> "Giving what does one give strength?
> Giving what does one give beauty?
> Giving what does one give ease?
> Giving what does one give sight?
> Who is the giver of all?
> Being asked, please explain to me."

> "Giving food, one gives strength;
> Giving clothes, one gives beauty;
> Giving a vehicle, one gives ease;
> Giving a lamp, one gives sight."

> "The one who gives a residence
> Is the giver of all.
> But the one who teaches the *Dhamma*
> Is the giver of the Deathless."

- *Saṃyutta Nikāya* 1:41-42

I affirm that the practices of giving and welfare work are the ultimate goal of Buddhism. The dynamism of the *Bhikkhunī* Order is most obvious in welfare work. It is transforming femininity into benevolence, and it transfers the merits of one to the salvation of others. That is to say, it fundamentally changes one's mindset from selfishly accumulating spiritual merit for oneself through self-cultivation to one of transferring or offering merit to others.

Modern welfare activities by *Bhikkhunīs* began with a Buddhist self-reliance organization founded in 1986 by the Buddhist nun Myohee (妙喜, 1935~2007) at Yaksu-sa Temple in Sinrim-dong, Seoul. The Buddhist Restoration Gongdeok Society opened a self-governing nursing home in October 1989 after securing land in Hwaseong, and the Society was incorporated in April 1991. In July 2004, the Society established a social welfare corporation, and today they are a model welfare organization operating a nursing home for the elderly and facilities for the disabled. On March 31, 2007 Ven. Myohee passed away at age 72.

One typical example of *Bhikkhunī* welfare work is Jungtosa-gwanjajaehoe, managed by Ven. Neunghaeng (能行) and located in Ulju-gun, Ulsan-si. In 1989, she founded the Amita Hospice Association, and in 1993, she began a system to provide professional hospice education. In 1997, she organized the Korean Buddhist Medical Care Association to educate professional caregivers. In 2000, the Jungto Village, the first independent Buddhist hospice center, was opened by Ven. Neunghaeng. And she opened the Jungtomaeul Jajae Nursing Hospital in June 2014, and provided an indicator of Buddhist welfare in terms of Buddhist practice and compassion as happiness community.

A typical *Bhikkhunī*-run welfare facility in downtown Seoul is the Mokdong Youth Center, which opened on October 26, 1988. It has become a great source of pride for local residents. Ven. Hyechoon (慧春) served as its first director begining in September 1988, and Ven. Gwangwoo (光雨) was the second. In January 1999, Ven. Myeongwoo (明又) had the center renamed Mokdong Youth Training Center, and it is now managed by Ven. Gyoungryun (暻輪).

The Daejeon Beopdong Social Welfare Center, which was established on March 19, 1993 and is now run by Daejeon's Daeduk Ward Office, is another outstanding welfare facility.

Buddhist welfare work, realizing the practice of social welfare / Inaugural assembly of the 'Korean Bhikkhunī Practitioners Welfare Association' (Jan. 21, 2016)

Annual event of compassion at the Korean Cancer Center Hospital, hosted by the Youngsan Seon Center

IV. **The Activities of** *Bhikkhunīs* **in Korea Today**

It was established with the aim of being self-sustaining and self-reliant to improve the quality of life of low-paid urban residents. Ven. Jongsil (宗實) was its first director and became security director in July 1996. Ven. Soohyeon (修賢) was evaluated as a community welfare representative through the operation of the Maehwa Comprehensive Social Welfare Center in Gunpo city in October 1997 and during his tenure as a director until 2007.

The Buddhist volunteer association founded in September 1994 by the abbot of Bangsaeng Seonwon, Ven. Seongdeok (性德), was responsible for systematic volunteer education and the efficient placement of volunteers to each welfare organization. In the early 1990s, the organization of volunteers was organized and the volunteer activities were carried out in welfare facilities.

Ven. Gyunghee of Daegu's Seobong-sa Temple currently operates the Hwaseong Nursing Home, and Ven. Beopsung of Seoul's Seongra-am Hermitage used to operate the Seongra-won Nursing Home (now closed). Seoul's Hyo-rim Won, another nursing home for the elderly, is operated by Ven. Moogoo (無垢). There are more than 30 welfare facilities operated by *Bhikkhunīs.*

One outstanding example of welfare work for the handicapped are Ven. Haesung and Ven. Eunsung who are trained in education through sign language. To help blind Buddhists, Ven. Jongshil established the Anayul Buddhism School and publishes Buddhist braille books for the blind. He is the first person to establish a *Dhamma* hall for the handicapped in Nowon-gu, Seoul.

Established in Daegu in 1985, the Buddhist Oriental Medicine Hospital is staffed by Buddhist nuns and nurses. It has a staff of about 30 including Ven. Jiseong. Ven. Hyedo, a professor of Joong-ang Saṅgha University, is taking the lead in the hospital's hospice care, and Ven. Yeohaeng of Seoul's Youngsan Seonwon is practicing voluntary sharing of cancer patients'. Ven. Jeongjin and many other *Bhikkhunīs* are active in the Buddhist Caregivers Association. On January 9, 1996, the Jogye Order's Social Welfare Foundation took over that association and expanded it into the Jogyejong Volunteer Center.

Nursery schools run by the *Bhikkhunī* Order do outstanding

work in the welfare field. In 2016, *Bhikkhunīs* devoted to Buddhist welfare formed the Korean *Bhikkhunī* Welfare Practice Society which officially launched on January 21. The purpose of the foundation is to take the lead in local welfare activities and to contribute to social welfare by promoting Buddhism and firmly establishing the status of Korea's *Bhikkhunīs*.

Upon the Society's inauguration, they declared the following:

"We will follow the Buddha's teaching of improving ourselves and benefiting others (自利利他). The essential nature and work of a bodhisatta is to improve his own character and then teach others. We will practice unconditional compassion (無緣慈悲) to save all sentient beings. Unconditional compassion is one of three types of compassion taught in Mahāyāna Buddhism. It is an absolute form of compassion based on the concept of emptiness, a state where there is no discernible difference between self and others. We will also practice the great compassion of the buddhas and *bodhisattas* which is based on the concept that we are all of the same fundamental essence (同體大悲). We do this to help realize the Buddha world where all sentient beings are happy together."

The Jogye Order of Korean Buddhism established its Buddhist Social Welfare Foundation on February 25, 1995 with the intention of helping people and acting as a lamp to attract alienated people by providing welfare assistance. Currently, the Jogye Order's welfare foundation has 179 facilities: 106 in the Seoul metropolitan area, 38 in Yeongnam, 23 in Honam, 10 in Chungcheong, and 2 on Jeju Island.

7.
Culture (文化):
Sharing Artistic Sensibilities is the Lubricant of Life

Here, culture does not mean a great cultural predicate of something that is typified as a lifestyle of a society or a group based on history, or a material or spiritual product. It is a field of the subject of the current activity of the *Bhikkhunīs,* and it refers to the value as a popular culture that everyone can understand and enjoy. It is like a song, a play, a picture, or an art that we often get through mass media or can easily get in touch offline. It is as if it is a hobby, but it is the case that it accomplishes its original purpose by demonstrating the utmost quality in this field.

The purpose of this essay is that the identity of the cultural activist pointing out here is the renunciant, and one's ultimate is the practice and edification of masses. For this reason, the pop culture and artistic sense of the *Bhikkhunīs* and the field activities are the means of various kinds of expedient edification for the sensitivity of the various masses.

Ven. Jeongyul (廷律) is a very popular Korean vocalist. She says:

> "The stage is my meditation room, and the song is my Zen (Seon) meditation, so the moments I sing on stage and the moments I pray in the temple are no different. They are both Buddhist practice."

Let's enjoy this song:

> Even darkness can be a light for a moment.
> With right thoughts and right actions
> I can clear the darkness and illuminate the universe.
> Now I can realize it in my heart.
> (refrain)
> Let's practice and practice
> Practice without retreat
> Like the Buddha did
> I can also be like Buddha
>
> Resentment exists just for a moment
> Everything can be grace with a grateful mind
> We can taste the pleasure of sharing.
> Now I can truly understand it as it is.
> (refrain)

Bhikkhunī Ven. Jeongyul sings a Buddhist hymn at Myeongdong Catholic Cathedral.

This is a special song titled "Like the Buddha Did", and I like this song very much. It is a song that contains the very essence of Buddhism. If you listen to it, you feel it resonate deeply in your heart. As we listen to music, our heart resonates, and music often becomes a symbol of our life. Sometimes I hear a song that seems to reflect my own situation.

The activities of *Bhikkhunīs* can also harmonize well with popular culture. As an independence activist during the Japanese occupation, Ven. Okbong (玉峰, 1913-2010), abbess of Donghak-sa Temple in 1967, is famous as a *Bhikkhunī* painter who specializes in Chinese ink paintings of bamboo (墨竹) and orchids (墨蘭). Her paintings have recently been attracting attention as a form of contemporary plastic art that combines performance art and Buddhist art. Other *Bhikkhunīs* active in the arts are: Vens. Hyedam, Soojeung, Beopseong, Guisan, Seonyoo, Muae, and others.

Ven. Dong-hee (東熙) is the most famous performer of *Yeongsanjae* (靈山齋, Intangible Cultural Asset No. 50, "Celebration of Buddha's Sermon on Vulture Peak") and is unrivaled in the field of *beompae* (Buddhist chanting). The list of *Bhikkhunīs* known for their singing is longer than in other

Beompae
(梵唄: Buddhist hymn praising the virtues of the Buddha)

artistic endeavors. They include: Vens. Jiseong, Beomjo, Myosim, Soobeop, Ogong, Moojin, Jeongjin, and others. Ven. Dasol is a Korean singer and Ven. Jeongyul is a vocalist and both are loved by the public.

Ven. Beophyun (法賢) promotes the teachings of Buddhism through beautiful music, both in temples and in prisons. Ven. Seoyeon (西蓮) is a senior flutist in the Masan City Symphony Orchestra and is the first *Bhikkhunī* to record a popular song titled "Indra." Ven. Jeonghaeng is also a talented soprano vocalist who graduated from Sookmyung Women's University and debuted at Carnegie Hall while studying in the United States.

A leading figure in the art of flower arrangement is Ven. Jiyeon (知衍). In 1983, she founded the Woodamhoe Association and Buddhist Flower Arrangement Research Institute at Giwon-sa Temple. In 1988, she also established the Korean Buddhist *Bhikkhunī* Flower Arrangement Association. Separately, Ven. Bomyung (寶明) formed the Yeonhwa Flower Association in 1988 and Ven. Jeongmyung founded the Flower[floral] Arrangement Association in 1991. Ven. Jeongmyung is also the chairman of the Korean Buddhist Paper Flower Transmission Association as a master of the paper flower arrangement.

As a *Bhikkhunī* active in the broadcasting industry, Ven. Jeong-mok (正牧) is very well known. A Buddhist TV program titled "The Melody of a Cup of Tea" received a grand prize for its broadcasting. Now she is contributing to making the world more beautiful by operating Yuna Broadcasting, a professional broadcasting service. Venerable *Bhikkhunīs* Jayong, Jinmyung and Il-eom were also noteworthy successors to Ven. Jungmok. Especially, Ven. wonwook of Mokdong's Banya-sa Temple in Seoul is a leading Buddhist broadcaster in Buddhist doctrine, and Ven. Neunghaeng is a specialist in hospice care and also a popular facilitator in the field of counseling.

In the ever-expanding field of temple food are *Bhikkhunī* specialists like: Vens. Daean, Hongseung, Seonjae, Hyowon, Eunwoo, Un-a, Woogwan and Seon-o. Ven. Jiyul (知律) made a name for herself as an environmental activist and founder of the Green Resonance Movement, a Korean environmental NGO. To protest the construction of a tunnel through Mt. Cheonseong-san as part of a high-speed railway, she went on a hunger-strike five times, two of which lasted 350 days.

8.
Organization (組織):
An Organization of Harmony and Compassion

Then the Blessed One addressed the *Bhikkhus* as follows:

> "*Bhikkhus*, there are six memorable qualities that create love and respect and are conducive to helpfulness, to non-dispute, to concord, and to unity. What are they?"

> "[The first is] when a *Bhikkhu* performs acts of loving-kindness both in public and in private towards his companions in the holy life. This is a memorable quality that creates love and respect and is conducive to helpfulness, to non-dispute, to concord, and to unity."

> "[The second is] when a *Bhikkhu* speaks words of loving-kindness both in public and in private towards his companions in the holy life. This is a memorable quality that creates love and respect and is conducive to helpfulness, to non-dispute, to concord, and to unity."

"[The third is] when a *Bhikkhu* thinks thoughts of loving-kindness both in public and in private towards his companions in the holy life. This is a memorable quality that creates love and respect and is conducive to helpfulness, to non-dispute, to concord, and to unity."

"[The fourth is] when a *Bhikkhu* shares things with his virtuous companions in the holy life; without reservation, he shares with them any gain of any kind that accords with the *Dhamma* and has been obtained in a way that accords with the *Dhamma*, including even the contents of his own alms bowl. This is a memorable quality that creates love and respect and is conducive to helpfulness, to non-dispute, to concord, and to unity."

"[The fifth is] when a *Bhikkhu* embodies both in public and in private possessing in common with his companions in the holy life those virtues that are unbroken, untorn, unblotched, unmottled, liberating, commended by the wise, not misapprehended, and conducive to concentration. This too is a memorable quality that creates love and respect, and is conducive to helpfulness, to non-dispute, to concord, and to unity."

"[The sixth is] when a *Bhikkhu* maintains both in public and in private possessing in common with his companions in the holy life that view that is noble and emancipating, and leads one who practices in accordance with it to the complete elimination of suffering. This too is a memorable quality that creates love and respect and is conducive to helpfulness, to non-dispute, to concord, and to unity."

"These are the six memorable qualities that create love and respect, and are conducive to helpfulness, to non-dispute, to concord, and to unity."

- *Majjhima Nikāya* 48 「*Kosambiya Sutta*」 1-6

Most of our lives, whether we it want or not, we are controlled by organization. Whether it is for school, work, or something else, we tend to congregate. Moreover, people often like to meet by choice for one reason or another. Excluding relatives, people are often brought together by things they have in common such as common interests, common background or a common purpose. Gatherings of people can be purely social or for a specific purpose. A religious group is no exception. Under the general heading of "Korean Buddhism" are about 350 official and unofficial Buddhist organizations, and the *Bhikkhunī* Order is one of them.

At the time of the Buddha, the *saṅgha* (僧伽, Buddhist monks, nuns and laity) was organized as a community of practitioners. Practitioners of asceticism often stayed in a nearby monastery. In the rainy season, they would stop their itinerant practice (遊行), which involved teaching and begging for alms, and hold a meditation retreat in a monastery. This was a period of intense uninterrupted meditation practice that was mandatory for monks in training. Originally, these retreats lasted three months, from the 16th day of the 4th lunar month to the 15th day of the 7th lunar month.

The story goes that one day some *Bhikkhus* got into a vicious and violent dispute.

The Buddha heard of this and called them together and said:

> "Bhikkhus, what are you thinking? When you take to quarrelling and brawling and insulting each other, do you on that occasion perform acts of loving-kindness in thought, word and deed in public and in private towards your companions in the holy life?"

- Majjhima Nikāya 48 ⟨Kosambiya Sutta⟩ 5

The Buddha went on to tell them that such behavior would only cause themselves harm and make them bitter. He then told them about the six qualities that induce charity.

Public life, that is activities within the organization, is maintained by the necessity or desire to achieve a common goal. The greater the number of people, the greater is the likelihood of discord. So, here, harmony and unity are a prerequisite. In particular, religious groups are expected to have more virtue than others because of the nature of their goal. That is why the *sangha* is expected to be a community of unity.

The reason members of the *sangha* should maintain the virtue of harmony in life is that "breaking the unity" is

Ven. Hyechoon (chairperson of the National *Bhikkhunī* Association) and fellow members visit spiritual patriarch Ven. Sungchul to celebrate the New Year (1987)

one of the five major sins in Buddhism and one the Buddha emphasized.

Let's take a look at the dynamism of the nuns who have established various community activities based on the six virtues (六和敬), the six ways Buddhist practitioners should live in harmony and be sensitive and caring toward each other:

First of all, it is the first thing to form a nationwide *Bhikkhunīs* meeting that represents the status and interests of *Bhikkhunīs*. The Nationwide *Bhikkhunīs* Association has its roots in Udambara Society, which was organized on February 24, 1968, as the first nationwide *Bhikkhunīs* organization after the liberation from Japanese colonialism at Cheongryong-sa

Temple in Sungin-dong, Jongno-gu, Seoul. The Udambara society has established the three point program:

① the construction of the *Bhikkhunīs saṅgha*,

② the rationalization of the missionary,

③ the welfare society.

At that time, the *Bhikkhunī* elected to the first president was Ven. Eun-young (恩榮), the abbot of Tapgol-seungbang, Bomun-sa Temple which is located at Bomun-dong in Seoul. Ven.Eun-young, together with her teacher Ven, Geungtan (亘坦) was the main character who created the Korean *Bhikkhunī* Bomun Order.

The Udambara Society was officially inaugurated in 1971 and its second president was Ven. Cheonil (天日) of Seokbul-sa Temple. During her tenure as president, Cheonil helped elevate the status of *Bhikkhunīs* who felt alienated from Korean Buddhism by the *Bhikkhus*. In addition, a Buddhist memorial service was held at Seokbul-sa Temple, and the Society's first charity event was held to raise funds for a children's mission.

On September 9, 1975, Ven. Ji-myung of Hwaun-sa

Hall of the National *Bhikkhunī* Association, construction was begun under the guidance of Chairperson Ven. Gwangwoo and opened in 2003.

Temple in Yong-in, Gyeonggi Province, was elected the third president of the Udambara Society. She was very active in organizing the Temple Support Society. Ven. Ji-myung was one of 13 *Bhikkhunī* disciples who inherited the *Dhamma* lineage of Uiseon (義善), the mother of Ven. Mangong (1871– 1946), a prominent *Bhikkhus* Korean Seon master of the early 20th century.

The Udambara Society held a general meeting on Sept. 5, 1985 at Seoknam-sa Temple. They changed the name of the Udambara Society to the Korean Buddhist Jogye Order National *Bhikkhunī* Association and elected Ven. Hyechoon (慧春) as its 4th president. Ven. Hyechoon served consecutive terms. On May 18, 1995, at the National *Bhikkhunī* Conference held at the Mokdong Youth Center, Ven. Gwangwoo (光雨) of Jeonggak-sa Temple in Seoul was elected its 6th president and then re-elected as 7th president on September 15, 1999. Ven. Gwangwoo secured the independence status of the *Bhikkhunīs* by holding a groundbreaking ceremony of the "National *Bhikkhunī* Association Temple Beopryoung-sa" on September 10, 1998, and by Opening ceremony on August 19, 2003, during her reign as president. Ven. Myungseong (明星) was elected as the 8th and 9th president and served from October 2003 to October 2011. On October 17, 2011, Ven. Myungwoo (明又) was elected as the 10th President in the election. On October 12th, 2015, Ven. Yukmoon (六文) was elected as 11th president.

The Association held its 9th regular general meeting on March 24, 2016. On May 3 of that year, the first "Conference of Elders" was held, and Ven. Myungseong (明星), a chairperson of Unmun-sa Temple, was elected its first president. Ven. Soohyun (修賢), Ven. Ilbeob (一法) and Ven. Undal (雲達) were appointed presidential aides.

Sakyadhita (World Women Buddhist Association) has been actively participating in Buddhist associations around the world and is also a good example of the dynamism of Korean *Bhikkhunīs*. With over 2,000 members in 45 countries, *Sakyadhita* focuses on uniting Buddhist women around the world, building an international Buddhist network, supporting Buddhist women's education, the growth and development of Buddhist religious retreats for women, and world peace based on Buddha's teachings. Sponsored by the Dalai Lama, it was formed in February 1987 in Bodogaya, India. The biennial World Women's Buddhist Conference has been held since 1987, when the first international convention was held in Bodhgaya, India, from June 23-30, 2015, to the conference held in Jakarta, Indonesia.

In 2004, Korea held the *Sakyadhita* International Conference, inviting more than 900 *Bhikkhunīs*, monks and Buddhists from around the world. '*Sakyadhita*' means the daughters of Buddha in Sanskrit. Some 2,000 monks attended the opening ceremony, while more than 1,500 appeared at the closing event, showing the importance and also the influence *Bhikkhunis* possess in the local Buddhist community. The Korean women's lay Buddhists including the *Bhikkhunīs* were held in Seoul from June 27 to July 2, 2004, and the Korean branch, *Shakadita* Korea, was launched on July 17, 2013.

Other Korean Buddhist organizations include: Seonmoon-hoe, Junghye-dorang, Mokryun-hoe, Bohyun-hoe, Geumryun-hoe and Yeongsan-hoe. There is also the Samso-hoe Society, an inter-religious fellowship organization supported by: Buddhist nuns of the Jogye Buddhist Order and the Won Buddhist Order and Catholic nuns.

Seonmoon-hoe Association is a friendship organization formed in May 2005 at Bakheung-am Seon Center, Yeongcheon city in order to establish discipline of *Bhikkhunī* Seon Center operation and pure rule discipline. It is made up of about 1,000 *Bhikkhunīs*, and is taking the lead in promoting the nationwide *Bhikkhunī* Seon Center and making friendships among *Bhikkhunī* monks.

Junghye-dorang was an organization consists of group of 63 people including mainly *Bhikkhunīs* gathered at Baekhwa-seonwon Zen center in order to reflect the interests of the *Bhikkhunīs* to the new constitutional law in 1994. On May 9 of the same year, the founding ceremony was held at the Samseon Missionary Center, and it was officially launched as a single organization to the Order for the interest of *Bhikkhunīs*.

Junghye-dorang invited professional staff of Zen (Seon) center, Sutta school, and Universities at that time, and started research committees of six fields (the Constitutional Law Team, the Postulant Education Team, the Sutta Education Team, the College Education Team, the Seon Center Team and the Social Welfare Team). And a reform committee (9 members including reform committee members, Ven. Yukmoon, and Seongchong, etc.) to reflect the *Bhikkhunīs'* interest in the constitutional law. However, the activities of Junghye-dorang could not achieve the goal because of the crisis consciousness of the *Bhikkhus* (the male monks), but the bold and unprecedented effort to secure the status of the *Bhikkhunīs* was highly appreciated.

Mokryun-hoe Association is a friendship group of the elder *Bhikkhunīs* of Seoul and Gyeongin area, and Bohyun-hoe Association is the friendship group of the young *Bhikkhunīs* who are affiliated to Seoul. The Geumryun-hoe was founded by the *Bhikkhunīs* of Busan and neighboring provinces for the purpose of cultivating the apprenticeship, and it helped the students to build the *Bhikkhunī* students Association of Dongguk University Gyeongju campus. Youngsan-hoe has been a social organization for Daegu area *Bhikkhunīs* Association.

Samso-hoe is a friendship group of the Buddhist *Bhikkhunīs*, Won Buddhism sister, and Catholic nuns. It is a social organization founded in April, 1988. Literally Samso means 'three laughing'. Here the 'laughing' symbolically means 'friendship' between the three religious group for the inter-religious dialogue. It has attracted great attention with fresh impression, such as holding Samso concert and Samso poetry festival and donating the proceeds (profit earned) to the social underprivileged.

It can be concluded that the present *Bhikkhunīs* order has been able to demonstrate their abilities to some extents in the field of the rationalization of the missionary, and the construction of welfare society in the three point program which was mentioned above. However, the construction of the gathering of *Bhikkhunī sangha* and the expansion of the *Bhikkhunī* suffrage still remain as the task to slove.

The Korean *Bhikkhunīs* have established a systematic, effective way of training new nuns. They begin with a novice period, progress to sutta study schools, and go on to meditation halls or other vocations of their choosing. The monastic life here is inspiring, although, as in other Asian countries, it is undergoing change due to the country's modernization and developments in the predominant Jogye Order of Korean Buddhism.

To understand Korean Buddhism and monastic life, it is helpful to remember that many influences, spanning over a thousand years, have brought Buddhism to where it is today. These include five hundred years of Confucian law, as well as Taoism, shamanism, and animism, which are still practiced in many temples. In recent years, Christianity also has influenced some city temples, which now have choirs, Sunday schools, and Christian-style religious services. Over time, Korean Buddhism and Korean *Bhikkhunīs* have absorbed these influences and evolved with their own unique flavor.

The *Bhikkhunīs* communities are independent from the *Bhikkhus*, although sometimes they reside on the same mountain. However, the monks and nuns may attend formal ceremonies, communal events, *Dhamma* talks, ordination ceremonies, and funerals together at a large temple. From time to time abbots and abbesses come together for annual training periods and discussion of the events at their temples. Apart from these instances of sharing, the nuns live separate, self-sufficient lives, with their own supporters, training schools and meditation halls, in thousands of temples varying in size from small hermitages to very large temples. They even have their own *Bhikkhunī* masters and "family" lineages. In the latter, disciples of the same master are "sisters", *Bhikkhunīs* who are colleagues of their teacher are "aunts" and so on.

The monks and nuns have similar life styles, temple organizations, robes, sutta schools, and meditation halls, although the *Bhikkhunīs* four-year sutta schools are more developed than those of the *Bhikkhus*. Because of this, the monks generally show respect for the nuns, especially those who are elder or positions senior to their own. The nuns also have a very strong meditation order, where in over thirty-five *Bhikkhunīs* meditation halls, twelve hundred or more nuns practice meditation almost continuously throughout the year.

The lineage of Korean *Bhikkhunīs* is not completely clear. We can discover in an old history log listing the unbroken lineage of abbesses in the history of Korean Buddhism. Queen Seondeok (善德 r.632- 647) of Silla founded the temple 1,350 years ago and became a *Bhikkhunī*. Historically an unbroken lineage of *Bhikkhunīs* continues to this day. Records

The Jogye Order of Korean Buddhism awards seven elder *Bhikkhunīs* 'celebrity precepts' in Vairocana Hall(大寂光殿) at Haein-sa Temple. They are: Vens. Hyewoon, Junghwa, Gwang-woo, Junghoon, Myoeom, Jiwon, and Myungseong.

Launch of the National Conference of Elder *Bhikkhunīs*,
executives pay homage to their elder *Bhikkhunīs* [2016].

IV. **The Activities of *Bhikkhunīs* in Korea Today**

in Buddhist libraries reveal descriptions of early ordinations even prior to this period and tell of the transmission of the Korean *Bhikkhunī* ordination to Japanese nuns. Many stories, too, have been passed down about various queens, many of whom became *Bhikkhunīs*, and their great works to support the *Dhamma*. It is suspected that although the *Bhikkhunīs* order did not die out during the Confucian rule or the Japanese occupation, the ordination procedures for both monks and nuns were simplified.

Nowadays, the most senior *Bhikkhunīs* are generally well known. They preside over the main rituals and ordinations and are the masters of their lineages or heads of major temples, sutta schools, or meditation halls. Sometimes they are simply known for being a devout, dedicated *Bhikkhunī* and may or may not have exceptional abilities. Not all of the senior *Bhikkhunīs* have many disciples, but they usually are part of a large "family" lineage, with many younger *Bhikkhunīs* following in their footsteps. The products of their work are found in the temples, sutta schools, and meditation halls they have constructed, as well as in their *Dhamma* teaching, translation work, and the role model of monastic life they set.

⑤

The Korean *Bhikkhunī Dhamma* Family Today

The *Bhikkhunī* order of today has grown into a dynamic organization since the Buddha first embraced women renunciants. Why have so many wise and talented *Bhikkhunīs* been largely overlooked and forgotten? And why do most Korean books about Buddha and his teachings deal almost exclusively with *Bhikkhus* and their achievements?

Part of the reason may be because *Bhikkhunīs* themselves have bought into Korea's male-dominated cultural trap, and they regard their subordinate status to *Bhikkhus* as a matter of course. And Korean culture today was primarily influenced by late Joseon neo-Confucian ideology that was extremely chauvinistic. In writing this book I had to research very deeply and meticulously to find even small traces of the impact *Bhikkhunīs* had on Korean Buddhist history because data was so conspicuously lacking.

In Buddhism, a *Dhamma* family consists of disciples of the

Sujeong *Dhamma* family's 7th patriarch, Ven. Queyoo, with his mother Ven. Gyeyoon and fellow practitioners (circa 1953). In keeping with Ven. Queyoo's vow, the first edition of *Sujeong Dhamma Family Lineage* was published in 1972 and was the first in *Bhikkhunī* history.

The Cheonghae *Dhamma* family is the earliest of Korea's *Bhikkhunī Dhamma* families. Its founders were Dohan (道閑) and Daeyoo (大宥) who received the precepts from Naong Hyegeun (懶翁慧勤, 1320–1376) at Yoojeom-sa Temple at the end of the Goryeo period.

same master who carry on a past patriarch's lineage. In Korea the concept of 'family clan' originated in Confucianism but was already common in Buddhism. The relationship between a teacher and a disciple is like this. An ordination teacher (得度師) permits shaving of renunciant and accepts as a student. A student is a disciple. The relationship between the Master and the Disciples is symbolized as 'Parents and Child'. Therefore, the most basic relationship that has formed the foundation of descendant is the teacher (master) and student (disciple). Based on this relationship, a genealogy was formed, and members of this lineage were gathered together to form a close group of fellow practitioners of the same school or master, which led to the birth of a *Dhamma* family (門中) or a fraternity of fellow

V. **The Korean *Bhikkhunī Dhamma* Family Today**

disciples of the same master.

It is a distinguished disciple, head monk, or senior disciple. There are a few more names for this in Korean according to the specific relations with the master, such as the precept disciple, the *Dhamma* disciple. The *Dhamma* heir, or the successor of the master: In this case master is also called *Dhamma* teacher (嗣法師) in Korean.

Dhamma lineages are the 'family trees' of the Buddhist tradition. *Dhamma* lineages usually begin with Sakyamuni Buddha and extend down through a line of Buddhist masters up to the present day. However, a Buddhist order, or a fraternity of fellow disciples of the same master adds one more thing. It is the implementation of a common good for individuals, denominations, and society. It means also the original function and role of the Buddhist order or unity (僧伽 *saṅgha*), which is interpreted as 'a group of good friends'.

The Buddha often uses the phrase "frined" when he calls disciples of the Buddhist order or unity. That means that the Buddha himself is not a divine being or a special being with the power of a savior or leader. They call it truly from the heart that goes hand in hand to walk the path of learning and practice of truth (law: *Dhamma*).

Let's take a look at the contents of one sutta (*Saṃyutta Nikāya*) that conveys the meaningful word of the Buddha in relation to it:

> Ānanda asked the Buddha:
> "Oh Buddha! Thinking that we good friends considered to be the fulfillment of the half of the sacred paths. How about this?"
> The Buddha replied:
> "Ānanda. Not like that. Having a good friend and being in good fellowship is all that is sacred. For good friends, good comrades, through which he can cultivate eight sacred paths (八正道 Eight Noble Paths) and further develop the eight sacred paths."
>
> *- Samyutta Nikāya* 45:2

The Buddha says that in order to reach liberation or *Nibbāna*, the following basic three poisons from which all other afflictions are derived should be eliminated: (1) desire, craving (*rāga*); (2) anger, aversion (*dosa*); and (3) nescience, folly (*moha*). They must be removed, which is possible by practicing Eight Right Paths. It is only possible through the eight types of practices used in conjunction with each other to attain enlightenment for oneself and to lead sentient beings to liberation. This, in a nutshell, tells me that being a forerunner of whether life is a success or not is a good friend.

The Buddha preached in one Sutta (*Sutta-Nipāta* 1:3):

> "We make a profit and depend on it.
> I can hardly see the friends who seek no benefit without condition.
> He who is bright only in his own interests can not be purified.
> Go alone, like the horn of a rhinoceros."

-Sutta-Nipāta 1:3 ⌈The Rhinoceros-horn⌋ 41

This verse tells the lesson that the people who live for the purpose of profit in the world are too hard to make good friends in this harsh reality. This is a passage to let you know where the Buddha's true teaching is.

Ānanda was so proud of his awareness of the importance of having a good friend in his own way, and the Buddha unexpectedly thought that it was wrong and answered it all. This word of the Buddha, in short, is not just half of a good life, it is all about it.

The Buddhist scriptures tell a lot about 'good friend' (*kalyāṇamitta*). In the morning when the sun comes up, there is a forerunner in the way that the east sky first glows first, then the glowing light emanates, and as we rise up the eight sacred paths. In other words, if you have a good friend, you can expect to learn about the eight sacred paths. Sometimes we call a good friend as '*doban*' (道伴 companion on the path), a fellow practitioner; co-practitioner; sisters and brothers in the Buddhist order (*saṅgha*); a companion on the way of enlightenment.

In this chapter, we will examine the present situation of the *Bhikkhunī Dhamma* family which forms one axis of the Korean Buddhist order. I will first identify the founder or first patriarch of the *Dhamma* family and outline its formation through its descendants. This chapter is only a concise introduction but will be meaningful to confirm the status of the Korean *Bhikkhunī* order today. Identifying the founder of a *Dhamma* family is not unlike identifying one's hometown and learning about one's roots.

The 'beginner's mind' originates with the first arousal of the desire for enlightenment. To make the resolve to attain supreme enlightenment is to arouse the intent to achieve enlightenment (發菩提心). *Bodhi* (菩提) is enlightenment. It is a transliteration of the Sanskrit/Pāli term *bodhi,* meaning

V. The Korean *Bhikkhunī Dhamma* Family Today

wisdom or awakening. It is the wisdom of the true awakening of the Buddha. It is the wisdom of having precise cognition of things as they are (如實知見 or 正見). Insight in accordance with reality allows one to know and see the reality of all things as the Buddha did.

The current status of the *Bhikkhunī Dhamma* families are roughly 10 or so, and the founder or first patriarch of the *Dhamma* family is established to organize the genealogy. Among the *Bhikkhunī Dhamma* families, Cheonghae *Dhamma* family (靑海門中) was the most earliest established one. After that, Gyemin (戒珉)· Beupgi (法起)· Samhyun (三賢)· Sujeong (水晶)· Bongrae (蓬萊)· Yukhwa (六和)· Silsang (實相)· Boun (普雲) · Ilyeop (一葉) and Bomunjong (普門宗) *Dhamma* family were established. In addition, even though their founders and patriarchs are not identified, several *Bhikkhunī Dhamma* families exist and succeed genealogy by the representative figures and temples such as Duock (斗玉)·Bongwan (奉琓) *Dhamma* family, Seoul Cheongryang-ri Cheongryang-sa Temple *Dhamma* familiy, Seoul Bomundong Mita-sa Temple Talgol *Dhamma* family, and Seoul Ocksudong *Mita-sa* Temple *Dhamma* familiy.

1.
Cheonghae *Dhamma* family
(青海門中)

The Cheonghae *Dhamma* family is the oldest among the *Bhikkhunī Dhamma* families. Its founders were Dohan (道閑) and Daeyoo (大宥) who received the precepts from Naong Hyegeun (懶翁慧勤, 1320–1376) at Yoojeom-sa Temple at the end of the Goryeo period.

They are both worshiped as founders and patriarch of the *Dhamma* family. In 1966, disciples of that lineage began to discuss forming an official Cheonghae *Dhamma* family genealogy, and on June 15 of that year, they met to begin research and compile data.

For the next nine years, meeting regularly, they collected and compiled data, and laid a foundation for the establishment

Main Temple of Cheonghae *Dhamma* family: Mt. Bulryung-san Cheongam-sa Temple Baengnyeon-am Hermitage in Gimcheon, Gyeongsang-bukdo province

of the Cheonghae *Bhikkhunī Dhamma* family (青海門徒會) on May 12, 1975 at Baengnyeon-am Hermitage of Cheongam-sa Temple.

Ten years later on Oct. 29, 1985, two of the representatives of Ven. Hyechoon (慧春) and Ven. Jangil (長一), along with 50 monks had an official meeting and declared the establishment of the Cheonghae *Dhamma* family. This is the birth of Cheonghae *Bhikkhunī Dhamma* family. Three years later, on the Day of Buddha's Coming, *the Genealogy of Cheonghae Dhamma family* was published to the world.

Main Temple of Cheonghae *Dhamma* family: Mt. Gaya-san Haein-sa Temple Yaksu-am Hermitage in Hapcheon, Gyeongsangnamdo province

After 30 years later, the representative of Cheonghae *Dhamma* family Ven. Sungil (性一, Abbot of Sinheung-sa Temple) published the drastically revised version of *the Genealogy of Cheonghae Dhamma family* on April 5, 2018

According to this revised version of *the Genealogy of Cheonghae Dhamma family*, the Cheonghae *Dhamma* family succeeded from the first two co-patriarchs Ven. Dohan and Ven. Daeyoo to the following branches. Ven. Dohan linage succeeded to the following four sub-branches: Mt. Bulryung-san Cheongam-sa Temple Baengnyeon-am Hermitage, Mt.

Surak-san Seokrim-sa Temple, Mt. Palgong-san Donghwa-sa Naewon-am Hermitage and Mt. Gapjang-san Yongheung-sa Temple. Among these four branches, Baengnyeon-am, Seokrim-sa Temple, and Naewon-am Hermitage lineages were succeeded to Ven. Dohan's first senior disciple Gyemil (戒密). Yongheung-sa Temple *Dhamma* lineage was succeeded to Ven. Dohan's second senior disciple Euimil (議密).

On the other hand Ven. Daeyoo linage succeeded to the Yaksoo-am Hermitage Haein-sa Temple linage without any sub-branches upto the present.

2.
Gyemin *Dhamma* family
(戒珉門中)

The Gyemin *Dhamma* family (戒珉門中) regards Gyemin (戒珉) as its founder, who became a Buddhist nun at Eunhae-sa Temple in Yeongcheon, Gyeongbuk province. According to the *Lineage of the Gyemin Dhamma Family*, Gyemin was originally a daughter of King Injo (仁祖 r.1623~1649). She came to Eunhae-sa Temple as a refugee during the Manchu war of 1636 but stayed at the temple even after the war. While practicing at Baekun-am Hermitage, she attained enlightenment and recited the following *Nibbāna Sutta* (涅槃經):

"All things are impermanent (諸行無常). This is the law of arising and passing away (是生滅法). When arising and passing

Main Temple of Gyemin *Dhamma* family: Mt. Gaya-san Haein-sa Temple Samseon-am Hermitage in Hapcheon, Gyeongsang-namdo province

away cease (生滅滅已), Cessation is peace (寂滅爲樂)."

Afterward, she went directly to Ven. Manhwa (萬化) and became a Buddhist nun, taking the *Dhamma* name Gyemin (戒珉).

Plans to establish an official Gyemin *Dhamma* family were arranged by Gyemin's 11th *Dhamma* descendent, Ven. Seongmoon (性文, 1895~1974) who opened the Banya Seon Center at Haein-sa's Samseon-am Hermitage. She hoped to see an official assembly of the Gyemin *Dhamma* family and the official publication of its lineage in her lifetime. On March 4, 1991, Ven. Seongmoon's disciples organized the Association of the Gyemin *Dhamma* Family after her death, and after ten years of study and investigation, the official *Lineage of the Gyemin Dhamma Family* was published on December 30, 2003.

According to this lineage, the Gyemin *Dhamma* family succeeded from Seungun (承雲) to Hakchun (學天) to Boryeun (普蓮) to Bokjeung (福增). Ven. Bokjeung (福增) had three disciples who were Ven. Junggong (定空), Wooyoung and Wongong (圓空). Ven. Junggong lineage now represents the Gyemin *Dhamma* family.

3.
Beopgi *Dhamma* family
(法起門中)

The Beopgi *Dhamma* family is a *Bhikkhunī* group that considers Beopgi-am Hermitage as its spiritual foundation. Their first, second and third patriarchs and all their *Dhamma* descendants became monks after practicing on Mt. Geumgang-san. The Buddhist belief in Beopgi *Bodhi*satta, whose spirit is said to dwell on Mt. Geumgang-san, also greatly influenced their decision to renounce the secular world.

Ven. Daewon (大願) was their first patriarch, and his disciple, Ven. Choonghyu, became their second. During the time of their third and fourth patriarchs, Ven. Cheogeum (處金) and Ven. Changseom (昌暹), their number increased greatly.

Main Temple of Beopgi *Dhamma* family: Mt. Gaji-san Seoknam-sa Temple in Ulsan Metropolitan City

The *Dhamma* descendants of Ven. Cheogeum (處金) and Ven. Changseom (昌暹) have expanded their *Dhamma* family and now consider the following four temples their centers of activity:

Seoul Sungin-dong Mt. Samgak-san Cheongnyong-sa Temple, Ulsan Mt. Gaji-san Seoknam-sa Temple, Seoul Ocksoo-dong Mt. Jongnam-san Mita-sa Temple (Geumsoo-am) and Daejeon Mt. Bomun-san Bokjeon-am Hermitage.

The first patriarch Ven. Daewon name appears in the history of Mita-sa Temple. Luckily we can see the chronicle of Ven.

Daewon in the *Jongnam-san Mita-sa yakji* (終南山彌陀寺略誌 The Short History of Mt. Jongnam-san Mita-sa Temple written by An jin-ho 1943). According to the book, Ven. Daewon seems to have lived roughly around the latter part of 18th century to the first half of 19th century.

The Beopgi *Dhamma* family started the foundation of the family when Ven. Inhong (仁弘) and Dojun (道準) opened the conference of *Dhamma* family at the Seoknam-sa Temple in 1972. After ten years preparation, the *Dhamma* family published *the Pedigree of Beopgi-am Dhamma Family* to the world in December 20 in 1984 and officially declared the birth of Beopgi-am *Dhamma* family. Ten years later *the Pedigree of Beopgi-am Dhamma Family* was reprinted and the revised and enlarged edition was printed in September 15, 2008.

4.
Samhyun *Dhamma* family
(三賢門中)

Ven. Yeompyung (念平) and Ven. Manseon (萬善) are revered as the founding patriarchs in the Samhyun *Dhamma* family. The two founding patriarchs lived around the middle period of 18th century. Ven. Yeompyung was the first generation and Ven. Manseon was the second generation of the Samhyun *Dhamma* family. Especially, under the Ven. Manseon's linage, there were four disciples, Ven. Jiseong (智性), Ven. Boktan (福坦), Ven. Bokchan (福賛), and Ven. Gyegwan (戒觀). This period of the prime time of the Samhyun *Dhamma* family.

These the third generation *Dhamma* discendents played a leading role the establishment and consolidation of the

Samhyun *Dhamma* family. Particularly the three Ven. Jiseong (智性), Ven. Boktan (福坦), and Ven. Gyegwan (戒觀) played a key role the consolidation of the Samhyun *Dhamma* family that they are called Samhyun (三賢 three worthies). So the name of this *Dhamma* family is called 'the Samhyun *Dhamma* family'. Another story about the origin of the name of the *Dhamma* family is that most of the disciples and temple supporters came from the three hermitages i.e. Mita-am Hermitage of the Donghak-sa Temple, Samseon-am Hermitage of Haein-sa Temple, and Yoonpil-am Hermitage of Daeseong-sa Temple. So they named the *Dhamma* family as Samhyun (三賢).

In 1960s, Ven. Suock (守玉, 1902~1966) summarized the pedigree of *Dhamma* family with her memory of *Dhamma* teachers in one page *changhoji*, traditional Korean paper made from mulberry bark (for doors and windows). That was a turning point to establish a *Dhamma* family. After 15 years later, Ven. Suock discussed fully about the pedigree of *Dhamma* family with fellow practitioners, Ven. Beophee (法喜, 1887~1975), Ven. Junghaeng (淨行, 1902~2000), and Ven. Injeong (仁貞, 1899~1978). at Sudeok-sa Temple in 1975.

The Samhyun *Dhamma* family gathered the additional informations about the family tree and published *the*

Main Temple of Samhyun *Dhamma* family: Mt. Gaya-san Bodeok-sa Temple in Yesan, Chungnam province

Bhikkhunī Yeompyung Samhyun pedigree in April 7, 1976. Even though the pedigree could not includes the detailed information, it was a big achievements to list up the *Dhamma* names of fellow practitioners of the same school or master. After 30 years later, the revised version of *the Bhikkhunī Yeompyung Samhyun pedigree* was printed in May 12, 2008 and the revised and enlarged edition was published next year in March 30, 2009.

V. **The Korean *Bhikkhunī Dhamma* Family Today**

5.
Sujeong *Dhamma* family
(水晶門中)

The Sujeong *Dhamma* family originated from an assembly of fellow practitioners on Mt. Songni-san's Beopjoo-sa Temple's Sujeong-am Hermitage, and Ven. Gwanseon (觀先) and Ven. Neunghaeng (能行) are revered as its founders. They and their *Dhamma* descendants mostly worshipped at Beopju-sa Temple's Sujeong-am Hermitage or became nuns, and they took the hermitage's name as their own.

In the 1970s their 7th patriarch, Ven. Queyoo (快愈, 1907-1974), and Ven. Taesu (泰守) began to compile the *Sujeong Dhamma family lineage* and it was published in 1972. Afterward, they held annual meetings to gather more detailed information

Main Temple of Sujeong *Dhamma* family: Mt. Songni-san Beopjoo-sa Temple Sujeong-am Hermitage in Boeun, Chungbuk province

and agreed to publish a more detailed revision which was published on September, 1992.

The assembly of fellow practitioners was held annually. They investigated and recorded ever flourishing *Dhamma* family's activities. On the basis of this investigation and record, the assembly of fellow practitioners gathered together at Sujeong-am Hermitage in November 2nd 1990, and decided to publish the revised and enlarged edition of the *Sujeong Dhamma family lineage*. Finally the enlarged edition of the

Sujeong Dhamma family lineage was published in September 1992, and the revised edition was again published in Feburary 2016.

According to the new revised edition, their 2nd patriarch, Ven. Neunghaeng (能行), had three disciples: Ven. Eung-un (應雲), Ven. Jung-an (正眼), and Ven. Sang-hak (上學). Ven. Eung-un became their 3rd patriarch and turned out ten prominent disciples. This was a turning point for establishing the Sujeong *Dhamma* family. Ven. Eung-un's ten disciples were: Ven. Jaeil (載日), Jaheup (慈洽), Dowon (道圓), Deokjin (德津), Silsang (實相), Byunhong (辯弘), Myoheung (妙興), Daejeon (大轉), Daeheun (大欣), and Ven. Daesoon (大順). Among them, Ven. Jaeil and Ven. Daesoon were the most prominent and active and played a key role in establishing the Sujeong *Dhamma* family.

6.
Bongrae *Dhamma* family
(蓬萊門中)

The Bongrae *Dhamma* family regards Yoojeom-sa Temple as its head temple. In terms of history and scale, it is the most famous of the four Temples on Mt. Geumgang-san, the other three being: Jangan-sa, Pyohun-sa, and Singye-sa Temple. Their 1st patriarch was Ven. Choeseon (最善) and Ven. Choesang (最祥) who both seem to have lived around the first half of the 19th century, The 6th generation family group Ven. Bongongdang (本空堂) Gyemyung (戒明, 1907~1965) and his great-grandfather Ven. Sadeuk (四得, 1862~1940) who provided the momentum for the establishment of the *Dhamma* family renounced and practiced here. That is also the reason why the title of the *Dhamma* family was adopted in memoration of them.

Main Temple of Bongrae *Dhamma* family: Mt. Kirin-san Seobong-sa Temple in Daegu Metropolitan City

According to the *Dongguk Yeoji Seungram* (東國興地勝覽), Mt. Geumgang-san has five different names according to the season: Mt. Geumgang-san (金剛山), Mt. Bongrae-san (蓬萊山), Mt. Yeolban-san (涅槃山), Mt. Poongak-san (楓嶽山), and Gaegol-san (皆骨山). The terms 'geumgang' (diamond) and 'yeolban' (*Nibbāna*) are Buddhist terms, and both names for the mountain are used at different times of the year. It is called Geumgang (金剛) in spring when all kinds of flowers cover the mountain, and it is called Bongrae (蓬萊) in summer when the valleys and peaks are covered in thick foliage. In winter when the leaves are gone and the bare rock is exposed, it is called Gaegol (皆骨). All mountains are also called Mt. Geumgang-san ('Geumgang' means 'Diamond' in the Diamond Sutta) because it is the spiritual mountain of Buddhism.

The primary supporter for establishing the Bongrae *Dhamma* family was lay Buddhist Park Sadeuk (朴四得) who donated substantial sums of money to the four temples located on Mt. Geumgang-san. He also contributed greatly to the construction of the *Bhikkhunī* practice site, Deukdo-am Hermitage (得度庵). His generosity was revealed during the restoration of Singye-sa Temple when Ven. Gyunghee (慶喜) and followers of the Bongrae *Dhamma* family visited the site and confirmed that his name was engraved on a 'memorial stone' in front of Manseru Pavilion.

On March 25, 1987, a full-fledged effort to establish the Bongrae *Dhamma* family was launched in memory of Ven. Bongong's death at Seobong-sa Temple in Daegu. The participants resolved to compile their *Dhamma* family lineage and held annual meetings afterward. They elected Ven. Gyunghee (慶喜) as head of the preparation committee. Twenty years later in early 2008, they published the *Yoojeom-sa Bhikkhunī Bongrae Dhamma Family Lineage.*

7.
Yukhwa *Dhamma* family
(六和門中)

In Buddhism, 'yukhwa' (六和) refers to the 'six ways that monks harmonize with each other' or 'six virtues Buddhists should practice to live in harmony'. They are as follows:

1. to be unified in respectful deportment (身和同住);

2. to be unified in chanting and speech (口和無諍);

3. to be unified in purpose and mind (意和同事);

4. to be unified in the practice of purity (戒和同修);

5. to be unified in views (見和同解);

6. to be unified in virtues (利和同均), which are: profit 利, deed 行, discipline 學, and generosity 施.

These are the most important virtues that both monks,

Main Temple of Yukhwa *Dhamma* family: Mt. Mansoo-san Mujin-am Hermitage in Buyeo, Chungnam province

nuns, and lay Buddhists should practice because creating disharmony is equivalent to Buddhism's 'five heinous crimes' that cause one to be reborn in hell. The Yukhwa *Dhamma* family upholds these virtues to maintain unity and solidarity, and that is where their family name comes from. Based on propriety and harmony among fellow practitioners, a *Bhikkhunī Dhamma* family emphasizes harmony among members to maintain the *Dhamma* family. It was the early period of 1980s. Finally the representatives of *Dhamma* family held the first official meeting in November 1983 at the

Main Temple of Yukhwa *Dhamma* family: Mt. Taehwa-san Magok-sa Temple Youngeun-am Hermitage in Gongju, Chungbuk province

Seokbul-sa Temple. Then they decided to unify the *Dhamma* family, and to publish the book on the lineage of Yukhwa *Dhamma* family.

The establishment of the Yukhwa *Dhamma* family started with a pledge of unity and harmony among family members at Seokbul-sa temple around the early period of 1980s. They later agreed to undertake the publication of the *Yukhwa Dhamma Family Lineage* in November 1983, which was published in March 1984. In April 2002, a revised and enlarged edition was printed which included information missing from the first edition.

According to the revised and enlarged edition of the *Yukhwa Dhamma Family Lineage*, the Yukhwa *Dhamma* Family regards Ven. Sangwoldang (霜月堂) Gukin (國仁) as the first patriarch who lived at the early and middle period of 18 century. Along with Ven. Sangwoldang Gukin (國仁), the second generation Ven. Sinamdang (信庵堂) Bohak (普學) is regarded as the founder of the Yukhwa *Dhamma* Family. Ven. Bohak three disciple i.e. Ven. Wolsim, Yeohak, and Wolhan. The period of these three disciple was the prime time of the Yukhwa *Dhamma* Family. These three disciples contributed greatly to the actual establishment of Yukhwa *Dhamma* Family.

If we take a look at the relationship between the main temple and branch temple, Elder disciple Ven. Wolsim line regarded Mt. Mansoo-san Mujin-am Hermitage in Buyeo, Chungnam province as head temple of their family group. The younger disciple Ven. Wolhan line regarded Mt. Taehwa-san Magok-sa Temple Youngeun-am Hermitage as head temple of their family group. The middle disciple Ven. Yeohak line also maintain their family group as of today. However, Ven. Wolhan family group is the most flourishing *Dhamma* family at the present.

8.
Silsang *Dhamma* family
(實相門中)

The Silsang *Dhamma* family took their name from their first patriarch, Master Silsang (實相), who had attained enlightenment at Sudeok-sa Temple's Gyunsung-am Hermitage. Master Silsang had come to Sudeok-sa from Mahayeon (摩訶衍) on Mt. Geumgang-san while practicing with her disciple Sundong (順同). They became the founders of the Silsang *Dhamma* family.

The Silsang *Dhamma* family flourished under the guidance of their third patriarch, Ven. Euiseon (義善, ?~1923), who was Master Sundong's only disciple. Ven. Euiseon had 13 disciples: Ven. Sungsu (性修), Ven. Dodeok (道德), Ven. Sunggak (性覺),

Main Temple of Silsang *Dhamma* family: Mt. Deoksoong-san Sudeok-sa Temple Gyun-sung-am Hermitage in Yesan, Chungnam province

Ven. Sungyoon (性允), Ven. Mansung (萬性), Ven. Sangjung (常淨), Ven. Sungwook (性旭), Ven. Hyejang (慧藏), Ven. Gakwon (覺圓), Ven. Eungju (應住), Ven. Jungwon (淨源), Ven. Manhye (萬慧), and Ven. Dooryung (頭龍). Actually this provided the foundation for establishing the Silsang *Dhamma* family, which is why they consider Ven. Euiseon their true founder. Incidently, Ven. Euiseon was the mother of the eminent Seon master Mangong Wolmyeon (滿空月面 1871–1946), a *Bhikkhu* and a leading Korean Seon master of the early 20th century.

On March 1, 1992, Abbess Soongsimdang (崇深堂) Myungsoo

(明洙, 1925~2013) of Yeonhwa-sa Temple on Mt. Samgak-san initiated the first Silsang *Dhamma* family meeting at Hwaun-sa Temple under the will of the 5th generation descendent Woljodang (月照堂) Jimyung (智明, 1921~2013) of Hwaun-sa Temple Seon center director and arranged to have their family officially recognized. They then decided to meet annually to pursue this.

On May 2, 1994, the Silsang *Dhamma* Association held a general assembly at the Daesung-am Hermitage of Beomeo-sa Temple, and on Buddha's Birthday in 2003, their official *Dhamma* family lineage titled the *Silsang Dhamma Family Genealogy* was published, making it official.

According to the *Silsang Dhamma Family Genealogy*, the Silsang *Dhamma* family regarded Mt. Deoksoong-san Gyunsung-am Hermitage, Mt. Myukjo-san Hwaun-sa Temple, Mt. Samgak-san Yeonhwa-sa Temple, Mt. Gaseup-san Mita-sa Temple, and Mt. Geumjeong-san Daesung-am Hermitage as main Temples. With these five main temples as the center, the Silsang *Dhamma* family have expanded their *Dhamma* up to the present.

9.
Boun *Dhamma* family
(普雲門中)

The Boun *Dhamma* family was established in memory of its first, second and third patriarchs, listed in order as follows: Boun-dang (普雲堂) Yoonham (允咸), Geumgang-dang (金剛堂) Seonyoo (善有), and Simwol-dang (心月堂) Jungyeup (靜燁). They all lived in the first half of 19th century and practiced at Syngye-sa Temple's Boun-am Hermitage on Mt. Geumgang-san.

On September 27, 1984, the subject of officially establishing the Boun *Dhamma* family was first discussed at a birthday cerebration for Ven. Sooin (守仁, 1899~1997) who led the family at that time. She's the one who emphasized the necessity of

Main Temple of Boun *Dhamma* family: Mt. Hogeo-san Unmun-sa Temple Cheongsin-am Hermitage in Cheongdo, Gyeongsang-bukdo province

pursuing this. Next year on April 9, 1985, the family held their first conference to pursue this matter at Mireuk-am Hermitage in Jinju. In August 1986, a first draft of the *Lineage of the Boun Dhamma Family* was prepared, but it was not published until 2008.

The 6th generation of the *Dhamma* family was led by Ven. Sooin who served three consecutive terms as abbess of Unmun-sa Temple (1955-1966). She contributed greatly to the foundation of Unmun-sa Temple which is located on Mt.

Hogeosan (虎踞山) in Cheongdo-gun (清道郡), Gyeongsang-bukdo province. It is the largest training center for *Bhikkhunīs* in Korea. At present, there are usually around 250 students in residence undertaking either three or four year training programs.

10.
Ilyeop *Dhamma* family
(一葉門中)

The Ilyeop *Dhamma* family is a *Bhikkhunī* lineage founded in memory of Ven. Ilyeop (Dhamma name 一葉, 1896~1971), a *Bhikkhunī* (original name Kim Wonju 金元周) who led the Korean women's rights movement for 40 years. She was one of the most influential figures in the fight for women's rights during the Japanese occupation. Other prominent leaders in the movement were Na Hye-seok, Park In-deok, and Shin Juli-a. They formed the women's liberation group called 'Cheongtaphoe' (靑塔會).

Ilyeop (一葉) became a *Bhikkhunī* in 1928 at Seobong-am Hermitage on Mt. Geumgang under the guidance of *Bhikkhunī*

Main Temple of Ilyeop *Dhamma* family: Mt. Deoksoong-san Sudeok-sa Temple
Hwanheedae Hermitage in Yesan, Chungnam province

Master Sunghye (性慧). She later received the precepts from
Mangong (滿空, 1871–1946), a leading Korean male Seon master
of the early 20th century. With this connection to Mangong,
Ilyeop is also considered to belong to the Deoksoong Family
lineage, the largest *Bhikkhunī* lineage in Korea.

In 1974, after the publication of her book *Until the End of
Future Lives* (2 volumes), many of her followers decided to
establish a *Dhamma* family association in memory of her.
In January 2001, they published a new edition of her book

titled *The Collected Writings of Il-yeop*, which included her first book and other articles she wrote in 1974. In December 2010, they launched the 'Kim Ilyeop Cultural Foundation' with Ven. Wolsong as chairperson. Its purpose is to carry on research and commemorative projects for the *Bhikkhunī* community more professionally and faithfully, and also to pass on the legacy of Ven. Ilyeop. The Ilyeop *Dhamma* family regards their head temple as Sudeok-sa, where she and her disciple Ven. Gyunghee (慶喜) stayed and practiced.

11.
Bomunjong *Dhamma* family
(普門宗門中)

Bomun-sa Temple in Bomundong, Seoul, is the headquarters of the Bomunjong *Dhamma* family. Their founding patriarch was Ven. Seolwoldang (雪月堂) Geungtan (亘坦, 1885~1980), a champion of the Korean Bomunjong Order (one of Korea's minor Buddhist orders).

The Bomunjong *Dhamma* family was founded in April 20, 1972 and is an independent *Bhikkhunī* order not under the Jogye Order of Korean Buddhism. They consider their 'spiritual patriarch' to be the Buddha's aunt, Mahāpajāpatī-Gotamī, the first woman permitted to join the Buddhist order in compliance with a request by Ānanda, one of Buddha's ten

Main Temple of Bomunjong *Dhamma* family: Bomun-sa Temple Seokgur-am in Seoul

primary disciples. Ven. Beopryu (法流) of Silla is regarded as the restoration patriarch of Bomunjong *Dhamma* family.

Ven. Seolwoldang Geungtan was the first Supreme Patriarch and the first executive chief of the Bomunjong Order was Ven. Eunyoung (恩榮, 1910~1981).

12.
Other *Dhamma* families

There are several *Bhikkhunī Dhamma* families whose founders and patriarchs are unknown, but their lineage follows representative figures and temples such as: the Duock(斗玉) and Bongwan(奉琓) *Dhamma* families; the Seoul Cheongryang-ri Cheongryang-sa Temple *Dhamma* familiy, the Seoul Bomundong Mita-sa Temple's Talgol *Dhamma* family and the Seoul Ocksudong Mita-sa Temple *Dhamma* familiy. Details of when and where they were established are largely unknown.

Glossary

❖ **Anāgāmin** 阿那含, 不還: non-returner; a practitioner of the path of the *sāvaka* 聲聞 who has fully severed the afflictions of the desire realm (the five lower-level bonds 五下分結; in the *AbhiDhammakosa-bhāṣya*, the afflictions removed in the Path of Cultivation 修惑 in the desire realm 欲界) and may be reborn into the form realm 色界 or formless realm 無色界, but will not again be reborn in this world of desire.

❖ **Anattā** 無我: Absence of self, non-self. The lack of existence of an inherent self, soul, or self, from the standpoint of Buddhist analysis. The empirical self is merely an aggregation of various elements, and with their disintegration it ceases to exist; therefore it has no ultimate reality of its own. This is one of the most important philosophical concepts in all of Buddhism, and is understood as having been one of the primary realizations attained by Śākyamuni in his enlightenment experience

❖ **_Arahant_** 阿羅漢: Also arhan; an enlightened, saintly man; the highest type or ideal saint in Hīnayāna in contrast with the bodhisatta as the saint in Mahāyāna liberated one. It is the fourth and final stage of Hinayana practice and the personal ideal of Theravada Buddhism. One who has reached the end of the fourfold Way and attained _Nibbāna._ It is also one of the ten names of the Buddha.

❖ **Baizhang Huaihai** 百丈懷海: (720–814) A highly influential Chan monk of the Tang dynasty who was born in Changle, Fuzhou 福州長樂. His surname was Wang 王 (or perhaps Huang 黃). He is said to have enjoyed visiting monasteries since childhood, and he became a monk at the age of twenty under the tutelage of Xisan Huizhao 西山慧照. He was fully ordained by the Vinaya master Nanyue Fazhao. Shortly after his ordination, he went to Lujiang 廬江 (in Sichuan 四川) to where he studied the scriptures. At that time, Mazu Daoyi 馬祖道一 happened to be propagating the _Dhamma_ in Nankang 南康. Baizhang studied closely with him and received the seal of his _Dhamma_ transmission. Later on, Baizhang established a Chan monastery on Mount Baizhang 百丈

山, where he formulated his influential set of pure rules 清規 and guided people in spiritual cultivation. He is famous for having established the system of supporting the monastery through working in the fields. He once said, "A day without work is a day without food 一日不作 一日不食."

❖ **Begging for alms** 托鉢: To carry an alms bowl, a metaphor for religious mendicancy. Going about begging in the village, or an act of showing the way of compassion and humility to lead sentient beings to enlightenment. It is also based on the philosophy of non-possession. In the early stages of development of the Buddhist *saṅgha* in ancient India, itinerant monks would obtain one meal a day (in the forenoon) by carrying their alms bowls past the homes of lay people and accepting whatever offerings of food were proffered. With the establishment of permanent monastic settlements, monasteries were allowed to accept food from lay patrons, store it, and provide regular communal meals for the monks in residence. In China and Japan, Buddhist monasteries received donations of arable land (worked by peasant farmers) and thus were sometimes able to produce their own food supplies or even put grains and oils on the market.

❖ **bhikkhu** 比丘: Buddhist mendicant monk: A male member of the Buddhist Order, who must observe 250 precepts. It originally meant "beggar." A a fully ordained monk (Skt. *bhikṣu*). Originally means 'one who begs for food.' The term was originally used in India to refer to the fourth stage of the brahmanistic life, wherein the householder would renounce the world, become a beggar and seek enlightenment. In Buddhism, it came to refer to a Buddhist (male) monk; a practitioner who has renounced the secular world and was ordained.

❖ **bhikkhunī** 比丘尼: A Buddhist nun. A fully ordained female member of the *saṅgha*. A female member of the Buddhist Order, who must observe 348 precepts. Tradition states that the Buddha's aunt, Mahāpajāpatī 摩訶波闍波提, was the first woman permitted to join the order in compliance with the request of Ānanda. In the fourteenth year after his enlightenment the Buddha yielded to persuasion and admitted his aunt and women to his order of religious mendicants, but said that the admission of women would shorten the period of Buddhism by 500 years.

❖ **Bodhisatta** 菩薩: Generally speaking, a Buddhist practitioner intent on the attainment of enlightenment based on profoundly altruistic motivations. *Bodhi* 菩提 (translated into Chinese as 覺) means 'enlightenment' and satta 薩埵 means 'living being,' thus, a being seeking enlightenment, or an enlightening being. The bodhisatta is the model practitioner in the Mahāyāna tradition, who dedicates his or her efforts to the salvation of other beings. This concept is used in Mahāyāna texts to distinguish from the earlier Indian notion of *arahant* 阿羅漢 — a being who also attains a form of enlightenment, but whose realization is considered to be inferior due to the selfish orientation of the practices pursued in its attainment. In this regard, the bodhisatta is said to possess two main characteristics that distinguish her or him from the arhat, and other inferior religious practitioners: a deep sense of compassion 慈悲 for the suffering of all other beings, and a special type of wisdom based on a realization of the nature of the emptiness (空: Pāli. *suññatā*, Skt. *śūnyatā*) of all existences. The bodhisatta attains his/her enlightenment by arousing the thought of selfless enlightenment (*bodhicitta*) and practicing the six perfections (*pāramitā* 六波羅蜜) based on compassion (*karuṇā*).

❖ **Dhammapada** 法句經: the *Dhamma* Phrase Sutta, or the Way of Virtue: A traditional collection of the teachings of Buddha. *Faju jing* (Pāli. *Dhamma*pada); title transliterated as 曇鉢經. 2 fasc. by *Dhamma*trāta 法救, T 210.4.559–574. Translated by Vighna 維祇難 et al. A collection of phrases comprising the basic teachings of Buddhist morality.

❖ **Dependent arising (or origination)** 緣起: Nothing in the whole phenomenal world exists independently of causal factors. Everything arises from conditions; there is nothing that arises out of nothing; there is nothing that arises of itself; and things do not come into existence through the power of an external Creator. Thus, there is nothing that is self-contained, independent, or which has its own separate and independent nature. It is the condition of relationship to something else resulting in arising or production. In the meaning of causal production, all phenomena are given rise to due to the mutual relationships of countless causes (*hetu*: 因) and conditions (*paccaya*: 緣) and are not independently existent. If all causes and conditions did not exist, no effects could come into existence. This is a basic Buddhist teaching common to all Buddhist sub-schools.

❖ **Dhamma** 法: (Skt. *Dharma*). Rendered into English variously according to the context as: truth, reality; thing, phenomenon, element, constituent, (mental) factor; quality The word *Dhamma* is originally derived from the Indic root *dhr*, with the meaning of that which preserves or maintains,'especially that which preserves or maintains human activity. The term has a wide range of meanings in Buddhism, but the foremost meaning is that of the teaching delivered by the Buddha, which is fully accordant with reality. Thus, truth, reality, true principle, law. It connotes Buddhism as the perfect religion. The *Dhamma* is also the second component among the Three Treasures (*tiratana*) 佛法僧, and in the sense of *Dhamma*kāya 法身 it approaches the Western idea of 'spiritual.'

❖ **Dhamma family** 門中: Another name for a Buddhist order, or a fraternity of fellow disciples of the same master.

❖ **Dhamma transmission** 系脈: *Dhamma*-lineage. Esp. *Dhamma* lineages of eminent Buddhist masters. *Dhamma* lineages are the 'family trees' of the Buddhist tradition. *Dhamma* lineages usually begin with Sakyamuni Buddha and extend down through a line of Buddhist masters up to the present day. Syn. 法脈, 系譜, 傳法.

❖ **Enlightenment** 得道: Realization of the Way (道), or attaining the truth or enlightenment; to attain enlightenment through upholding the precepts, practicing meditation, and cultivating wisdom. In other words, it means realization of impermanence and selflessness of all phenomena in the whole universe. When the man of enlightenment contemplates, he sees all the phenomena as pure and complete. His insight sees the changeless within the ever-changing and identifies with both. He sees multiplicities or diversities in their essential unity. He who comprehends the unity within multiplicity and changelessness within the ever-changing, and becomes an integral part of both processes can be called a man of enlightenment.

❖ **Entering the monastic life** 得度: Taking ordination. a name of ceremony in which a Buddhist monk is ordained. It also means attaining perfection or Paramita beyond the sea of suffering. Upon entering into the Buddhist priesthood, one's head is shaved and a dyed robe is put on. To enter the monastic life. Ordination rites always involve receiving precepts 受戒, which 'enable' one to successfully follow the Buddhist path. The character 度 is originally synonymous with its graphic relative 渡, which means to 'cross over' esp. from 'this shore' of delusion to the 'other shore' of enlightenment—to cross over the flow of *saṃsāra*. Be careful not to confuse it with"attainment of enlightenment or truth"above which is pronounced the same in Korean.

❖ **Expedient means** 方便, 善巧方便: A method, means; skill-in-means; expedient means. A method that is convenient to the place, or situation,—opportune, appropriate. A skilful device, skilful means, expedient means, an artful liberative technique, an inconceivable skill in liberative technique, a temperamental convenience, a device or a temporary means to achieve an end, or leading sentient beings to the truth. It is an ingenious method of the Buddha and *Bodhisattas* to deliver all living beings according to their temperaments, vessels, or capabilities."If wisdom is the mother of enlightenment, an artful liberative technique is the father of enlightenment, "the sutta says.

❖ **Five aggregates** 五蘊: The five khandhas. Also translated into Chinese as 五陰 and 五衆. Khandha 蘊 means 'accumulation.' The collection of the five compositional elements of our existence. The five khandhas are a classification of matter and mind into five categories, which are form, feeling, perception, impulse and consciousness.

1. 'Form' 色蘊 (*rūpa*) is matter in general, the body or materiality.
2. 'Feeling' 受蘊 (*vedanā*) is receptive or sensory function.
3. 'Perception' 想蘊 (*saññā*) refers to images that surface in the mind.
4. 'Impulse' 行蘊 (*saṅkhāra*) is will, intention, or the mental functionthat accounts for craving. The power of formation potential. It isalso understood as all of the general mental functions not includedin the skandhas

of feeling or perception.

5. 'Consciousness' 識蘊 (*viññāṇa*) is the cognitive, or discriminating function. Knowing through discrimination (*pañca-khandha*).

The first is physical, the other four mental qualities; (2), (3), and (4) are associated with mental functioning, and therefore with 心所; (5) is associated with the faculty or nature of the mind 心王 manas.

❖ **Five obstructions (hindrance)** 五蓋: Five obstructions of wisdom; also written 五盖. Five kinds of affliction that block off the true mind: desire 愛貪 (*Kamacchanda*), wrath 瞋恚 (*vyapada* or 瞋怒: *paṭigha*), dullness 沈 (睡眠, *middha*), agitation and remorse 掉擧 (*uddhacca-kukkucca*), and doubt 疑 (*vicikiccha*).

❖ **Four accesses and four realizations** 四向四果: The four accesses and 'four realizations' of the *sāvaka* path):

1. 須陀洹 'stream-enterer' (預流); A transliteration usually rendered in English as 'stream-winner', or 'stream-enterer' (Pāli. *sotāpanna*). It is the first of the four realizations 四果 of the *sāvaka* 聲聞 path, which eventually leads to the level of *arahant* 阿羅漢.

2. 斯陀含 'once-returner' (一來);

   Transliteration usually translated into Chinese as 一來, 一往來, or 一往來果. A religious practitioner who will only be reincarnated in this world or in one of the heavens one more time. The second of the four lesser vehicle 小乘 realizations 四果. In the AbhiDhamma tradition, this practitioner is said to have eliminated the upper six kinds of nine levels of perceptual disturbances 思惑 in the desire realm 欲界 (Pāli. *sakadāgāmi*).

3. 阿那含 'non-returner' (不還, 不來); (Pāli. *anāgāmi*). A practitioner of the path of the *sāvaka* 聲聞 who has fully severed the afflictions of the desire realm and may be reborn into the form realm 色界 or formless realm 無色界, but will not again be reborn in this world of desire. This indicates the attainment of the third of the four stages 四向四果, which is that of freedom from rebirth in the desire realm.

4. 阿羅漢 '*arahant*' (無學): The highest type or ideal saint in Hīnayāna in contrast with the bodhisatta as the saint in Mahāyāna. He/she has eliminated all afflictions and reached the stage of not needing any more training 無學 (不學). In early Indian texts, the stage of arhat is the final goal of Buddhist practice—the attainment

of *Nibbāna*.

❖ **Four pairs and eight categories** [of *sāvaka* practitioners] 四雙八輩: The four pairs of stages, i.e. the eight stages to be attained by a practitioner of the arhat path—also commonly termed as 四向四果. These consist of different stages, each having two divisions. Four stages are states of attaining, and four are states of having attained:

1. *sotāpanna* 預流. Entrance into the stream of sanctification.
   i. 預流向. The stage of entering the stream of sanctification. ii. 預流果, stage of having entered into the stream of sanctification.

2. *sakadāgāmi* 一來 One more returning. i. 一來向 The state of attaining a state of one more returning. ii. 一來果 The stage of having attained a state of one more returning.

3. *anāgāmi* 不還 Non-returning. i. 不還向 stage of attaining a state of nonreturning, ii. 不還果 The stage of having attained a state of nonreturning.

4. *arahant* 阿羅漢 Perfect personality. i. 阿羅漢向. The stage of attaining *arahant*-ship. ii. 阿羅漢果 the stage of having completed *arahant*-ship.

❖ **Fourfold community** 四部大衆: The *sangha*. The four

groups of Buddhist followers: male/female monks and male/female lay people. The fourfold assembly or community, or the fourfold retinue: *Bhikkus* or monks, *Bhikkunis* or nuns, laymen and laywomen.

❖ **Ganhwa seon** 看話禪: Chan/Seon/Zen meditation method that seeks direct attainment of enlightenment through investigation of the 'keyword' (Ch. huàtóu; K. hwadu, 話頭). This Chan approach was first popularized by the Chinese Linji 臨濟 monk Dahui 大慧, who taught this method to be superior to the competing Caodong 曹洞 approach to meditation, known as 'silent illumination meditation' 默照禪. Throughout the subsequent history of East Asian Buddhism, phrase-observing meditation would be associated with Linji/Imje/Rinzai, while silent illumination became the main method of Caodong. 看 means 'to see' and 話 means a question. Here 'seeing,' means for the practitioner to probe deeply into the doubts in his own mind, as the key word points to the place where thoughts arise. In Korean Seon it is often applied as a synonym for gong-an 公案, but precisely speaking, the two are different. While gong-an refers to an entire exchange, usually a dialogue between Master and student, hwadu refers to the core issue. Originally in China gong-an meant a precedent in a public case, while in Chan/Seon/Zen training it refers to a realized teaching pointing to the nature of ultimate reality.

❖ **gong-an** 公案: The term was appropriated by Chinese Chan 禪宗 Buddhism, where it was used to refer to a specific Buddhist meditation device, distinguished from the traditional Indian Buddhist forms of meditation such as *samatha/vipassanā* 止觀. Gong'an meditation (in the West, more commonly known by the name of its Japanese rendering, *kōan*) usually consists of the presentation of a problem drawn from classical texts, or from teaching records and hagiographies of Tang and Song period Chinese Chan masters. After the case is presented, a question is asked regarding a key phrase (話頭) in the story, which usually presents a position that contradicts accepted Buddhist doctrinal positions or everyday logic. Its purpose is not to elicit a rational answer, but to serve as a focal point for a dynamic form of contemplation, which results in a nondualistic experience. After being developed in China, this practice spread to Korea as gong-an, where it has remained a prominent form of meditation in Korean Seon schools (mainly Jogye 曹溪宗) down to the present. In Japan, kōan meditation has been practiced mainly by the Rinzai school 臨濟宗, although certain Sōtō 曹洞宗 teachers like Dōgen 道元 did acknowledge the practice. Gong'ans are contained in edited collections, two of the most popular of which are the Wumen guan 無門關 and the Biyan lu 碧巖錄.

❖ **hwadu** 話頭: The 'critical phrase,' 'principal theme,' of the larger gong'an/kōan/gong-an exchange. The classic example is the longer gong'an, "A monk asked Zhaozhou 趙州,' Does a dog have buddha-nature 佛性, or not? 'Zhaozhou answered,' It doesn't have it (wu/mu/mu 無)'" (more commonly translated as 'no'). 〔無門關 T 2005.48.292c23〕 The gong'an is the whole exchange, the huatou/watō/hwadu is the word wu/mu/mu. The huatou is the focus of a sustained investigation, via a more discursive examination of the question, "Why did Zhaozhou say a dog doesn't have the buddha-nature when the answer clearly should be that it does?, "which is called 'investigation of the meaning; 'this investigation helps to generate questioning or 'doubt,' which is the force that drives this type of practice forward. As that investigation matures, it changes into a non-discursive attention to just the word 'no' itself, which is called 'investigation of the word' 看話 (Ch. kanhua) because the meditator's attention is then thoroughly absorbed in this 'sensation of doubt.' This type of investigation is said to be nonconceptual and places the meditation at the 'access to realization,' viz. 'sudden awakening.' The most sustained treatment of the use of huatou in Chan/Zen/Seon meditation appears in the Korean tradition and 'Keyword Meditation' (ganhwa Seon 看話禪) remains the principal type of meditation practiced in contemporary Korean Buddhism.

❖ **Han Yong-un** 韓龍雲: (1879–1944) Prominent Korean monk, poet, and writer. Also more popularly known as Han Yong-un 韓龍雲 or Manhae 卍海. In 1896, when Han Yong-un was 16, both his parents and his brother were executed by the state for their connections to the Donghak Rebellion 東學革命. He subsequently joined the remaining forces of the Donghak Rebellion and fought against the corrupt government, but was forced to flee to Oseam hermitage in Mt. Sorak. In 1905, he was tonsured by Yeon-gok 蓮谷 at Baekdamsa and was ordained by Yeongje 泳濟. There he studied many suttas In 1908, as one of the 52 representatives for the monasteries throughout the country, he participated in the establishment of the Wonjong 圓宗 and its headquarters at Wonheungsa 元興寺. After his return from Japan, where he witnessed the modernization of Buddhism at work, he wrote an article in 1909 arguing for the reformation of Korean Buddhism entitled, the Joseon bulgyo yusinlon 朝鮮佛敎維新論. He participated in Korea's fight for independence after Korea was annexed by Japan in 1910. In opposition to the Korean monk Hoegwang Saseon's 晦光師璿 attempt to merge the Korean Buddhist Order (Wonjong) with the leading Japanese Buddhist Orders such as the Sōtōshū 曹洞宗, Han Yong-un helped Seongwol 惺月 and others establish the Imje jong 臨濟宗 and its headquarters at Beomeo-sa in Busan. In 1919, he actively participated in the May First Movement and signed the Declaration of Independence as a representative of the Buddhist community. As a result he was given a three year sentence by the Japanese colonial government. In prison he composed the Joseon dongnip ui seo. In

1925, three years after he was released from prison, he published a book of poetry called, *Nim ui chimmuk*, and became a leader in resistance literature. In 1930, he published the monthly journal, *Bulgyo*, through which he attempted to popularize Buddhism and to inform the public of the need for independence. He continued to write and fight for independence until his death in 1944 at the age of 66, unable to witness the independence of Korea a year later on August.

❖ **khandha** 蘊: Cluster; aggregates. There are two main meanings: that of something that is accumulated and that of something differentiated. The constitutional elements (aggregates) of human existence, numbered at five 五蘊. The *khandhas* refer only to the conditioned world, not to the unconditioned 無爲

❖ **Lineage of the transmission of the precepts** 戒脈: Traditionally understood as having originated with Sakyamuni, transmitted through Mahā-Kassapa, down to the present-day recipients of the precepts.

❖ **Liberation** 解脫: Salvation; release, deliverance, setting free, emancipation, escape. Escape from bonds and the obtaining of freedom, freedom from transmigration, from *kamma*, from illusion, from suffering; it denotes *Nibbāna* and also the freedom obtained in *jhāna*-meditation. The mind becoming free from afflictions. Awakening to reality; breaking attachment. The peaceful condition resulting from escaping the suffering and vexation of the world. *Nibbāna*. Non-attachment to self.

❖ **Mahāyāna Buddhism** 大乘佛教: A translation of the Sanskrit term mahā-yāna 大乘, the name attached to a late Indian sectarian movement that became the main form of Buddhism in East Asia. The term was created together with the disparaging hīnayāna 小乘, which was used by the former group to distinguish the two. In the polemical sense, the concept of great vehicle (大乘)' refers to the fact that the Mahāyāna group considered their doctrines to be more open and universalistic in advocating that enlightenment was something attainable by all sentient beings, rather than just by the monks and nuns who practiced in the pure environment of the monastery. This movement produced a large body of new suttas, in which their new model practitioner, the bodhisatta 菩薩, preached the doctrine of the emptiness 空 of all things.

❖ **Merit transference** 廻向: To transfer merit; to offer one's merit 功德 to others, to the Buddha-nature, to the three Jewels, to thusness, etc. (Pāli. *pattidāna*; Skt. *pariṇāmanā*). To devote one's merits to the salvation of others. To fundamentally change one's orientation away from the selfish accumulation of merit gained by one's self-cultivation and offer it to someone or something other than oneself.

❖ **Middle way (Or middle path)** 中道: A term for the Buddhist path. In the earliest stratum of Buddhist literature it refers to a path that avoids the extremes of asceticism and self-satisfaction (*Pāli. majjhimā paṭipadā; Skt. madhyama-pratipad*). Later, during the development of Mahāyāna Buddhism, especially as taught by Nāgârjuna 龍樹 and others, it refers to the cultivation of the enlightened mindfulness which is not trapped in the extremes of nihilism or eternalism, or being and nonbeing. This 'mean' is found in a third principle between the two, suggesting the idea of a realm of mind or spirit beyond the terminology of 有 or 無, substance or nothing, or, that which has form, and is therefore measurable and ponderable, and its opposite of total nonexistence. Also used as an informal term to refer to the Madhyamaka 中觀派 school, which was founded by Nāgârjuna.

❖ **Nibbāna**涅槃: Extinction. As a verb, to enter extinction. An approximate transliteration of the Indic vulgar *Nibbāna*, which becomes the Pāli *Nibbāna* (Tib. mya ngan las 'das pa). Interpreted as the condition where the flames of delusion have been blown out—the final goal and attainment in Indian religions. In Hinduism, *Nibbāna* is the extinction of worldly desires and attachments, so that the union with God or the absolute is possible; absolute extinction or annihilation, complete extinction of individual existence.

❖ **Order** 宗團: A monastic order, or an organization of a Sect.

❖ **Ordination** 受戒: Receiving the precepts prescribed by the Buddha. To receive, or accept, the precepts, or rules; a disciple; the beginner receives the first five, the monk, nun, and the earnest laity proceed to the reception of eight, the fully ordained accepts the ten. In principle three leaders and seven witnesses are required on this occasion.

- ❖ **Ordination platform** 戒壇: The altar at which the precepts are received by the novice; the Mahāyāna altar is 方等戒壇

- ❖ **patriarch** 祖師: A first teacher, or leader, founder of a school or sect—a patriarch. A deceased member of the Chan/Seon/Zen lineage; usually one whose *Dhamma* descendants (heirs in subsequent generations) are still flourishing at present.

- ❖ **patriarchal Chan** 祖師禪: The Chan/Seon/Zen Buddhism understood as being initially transmitted from Bodhidhamma to the sixth patriarch Huineng 慧能. Also known as the Chan of the five houses 五家 and seven schools 七宗. As distinguished from Tathāgata Chan 如來禪, received directly from the Buddha.

- ❖ **Patimokkha** 波羅提木叉: Transliteration of the Pāli, *code of Vinaya precepts* (Pāli. *pātimokkha*); translated into Chinese as 戒本; literally means 'liberation from all afflictions.' In the traditional Indian vinayas it refers to the body of precepts to be kept by monks and nuns, specifically, a part of the Vinaya that contains the 227 disciplinary rules for monks and 348 nuns that is recited at every *uposatha* 布薩 ceremony. At this ceremony, every monk or nun must confess any violations of these rules. These are traditionally divided up into the eight groups. In China, the *pātimokkha* most often used was one associated with the Vinaya of the *Dhamma*guptakas 法藏部, which was rendered into Chinese as the Four Part Vinaya 四分律; it contained 250 moral precepts for monks. Over time, however, there were efforts in China to replace the 'Hīnayāna' *pātimokkha* with a 'Mahāyāna' one that could be used in rites of confession.

- ❖ **Practice** (修行, 修禪): Cultivation, or practice of *samatha* or meditation. Practicing the path of enlightenment, or cultivating the mind for attaining enlightenment and wisdom. To perform, practice, cultivate; to apply oneself to yoga/meditation practice. To practice meditation. To practice Zen meditation.

❖ **Precepts** 戒: Behavioral discipline; moral discipline; morality ; also written as 戒律. The rules of religious discipline, transliterated into Chinese as 尸羅 (*sīla*). Warnings, precautions, precepts, prohibitions, disciplines, rules. In Buddhism, practice of the precepts is one of the 'three practices' 三學 and one of the six perfections 六波羅蜜. It is the aspect of the Buddhist teachings which focuses on the nurturance of morality. Many Mahāyāna texts list the practice of the precepts as the most fundamental practice, after which one may engage properly in the practice of *samādhi* 定 (concentration) and *paññā* (wisdom) 慧.

There are various sets of rules provided for practitioners who are engaged in various degrees of commitment to Buddhism, at various levels, and from the perspective of differences in gender. For example, there are the five basic precepts for lay practitioners 五戒, the eight 八戒, the basic ten for monks and nuns 十戒, and the full set for monks 具足戒. Those for a nun are 348, commonly called 500. The precepts in Mahāyāna are defined primarily in the Brahmā's Net Sutta which gives the ten grave precepts (Esoteric Buddhism also has ten grave precepts) 十重戒, and forty-eight minor precepts. Buddhism has a variety of pairs of precepts, listed under 二戒.

❖ **Renunciation** 出家: Renunciation of the secular life to become a monk, join the monastic order, or receive ordination. Literally, to 'leave home' and become a monk or nun. In other words, to enter the Buddhist monastic system. The purpose of leaving home is to allow the believer to leave behind all worldly distractions and concentrate his/her full energies on the practice of the Buddhist path. The world-renunciant practitioner stands in contrast to the 'lay practitioner' 在家, who attempts to conduct his or her Buddhist practice while continuing to meet worldly responsibilities. A monastic, a renunciant.

❖ **Retreat** 安居: A meditation retreat. A period of intensified practice in the life of a monastery during which uninterrupted residence is mandatory for registered monks in training. 安居 means 'tranquil' 安 'shelter' 居. A more formal name is 'retreat in which the rules are bound' 結制安居. Originally the rainy season of three months, from the 16th of the 4th to the 15th of the 7th month, during which monks stay in their monasteries, concentrating on study and practice.

❖ **samādhi** 三昧: A high level of meditative concentration; mental training through meditation; the skillful unification of mind and object; the mental equanimity conducive to and derived from attention perfectly focused on its object.

❖ **Saṅgha** 僧伽: The Buddhist order or community: Lit. "amity" and "host," or "harmonious unity." The Buddhist community, or the fourfold community. The third of the Three Jewels of Buddha, *Dhamma*, and *Saṅgha*. A transliteration of the Sanskrit/Pāli. The community of monks and nuns—Buddhist practitioners who gather together in the common effort of attaining Buddhahood. In its original technical usage, it refers to a group of more than three monks. The term can be used just to refer to monks—including fully ordained monks (*bhikkhu*) and nuns (*bhikkhunī*) and novice monks(*sāmaṇera*) and nuns (*sāmaṇerī*)—or it can also include laymen(*upāsaka*) and women (*upāsikā*) who have taken the vows of 'individual liberation' (Skt. *pātimokkha-saṃvara*). One of the Three Treasures 三寶.

❖ **Samguk sagi** 三國史記: *History of the Three Kingdoms*. Compilation completed in 1146 by Gim Busik 金富軾. A work that treats the history of the three Korean kingdoms of Silla, Baekje, and Goguryeo, which includes much information on Buddhist figures.

❖ **Samguk Yusa** 三國遺事: *Legends and History of the Three Kingdoms*: The *Samguk Yusa*, 5 fasc.; T 2039. Written during the Goryeo by the monk Iryeon 一然 (1206–1289). A collection of stories related to the transmission and development of Buddhism in Korea, especially focusing on the Three Kingdoms and Silla periods. This text is a fundamental work for the study of the history of Korean Buddhism.

❖ **Saṃsāra** 輪廻: Transmigration. The original meaning of *saṃsāra* is 'flow together,' thus also translated as 流轉 as well as 'birth-and-death'. This is the expression of the ancient Indian idea that all living things repeatedly pass through life and death. Like a continually spinning wheel, sentient beings are reincarnated and die without end. In Buddhism, one is said to transmigrate through the triple realm 三界 (desire 欲界, form 色界 and formless realms 無色界) and the six destinies 六道 (god 天上, demigod 修羅, human 人間, animal 畜生, hungry ghost 餓鬼, hell-being 地獄).

❖ **Six ways that Buddhist practitioners should live in harmony** 六和敬: six ways that Buddhist practitioners should live in harmony and be sensitive and caring towards each other

1. to be unified in their respectful deportment 身和敬;
2. to be unified in their chanting 口和敬;
3. to be unified in their purpose 意和敬;
4. to be unified in their practices of purity 戒和敬;
5. to be unified in their view 見和敬;
6. to be unified in their benefits 利和敬, which refers to profit 利, deeds 行, discipline 學, and generosity 施.

There are other sets of six listed in other texts. See also 和敬. Also called the 六合念法, 六和合, and 六和. [大乘義章 T 1851.44.695c25]

❖ **Solitary realizer** 獨覺: Self-enlightened one. Self-enlightened one, etc. (pacceka-buddha). In the early translations it was rendered yuanjue 緣覺, i.e. enlightened through contemplation of dependent arising, especially as defined in the twelve nidānas 十二因緣. Later it was rendered 獨覺—individually enlightened—one who lives apart from others and attains enlightenment alone, or for himself, making a contrast with the altruism of the bodhisatta.

❖ **Southern Buddhism** 南方佛教: The line of transmission of Buddhism through South Asia after the time of King Asoka. This transmission proceeded from southern India and Sri Lanka (Sri Lanka), to Burma (Myanmar), Thailand and Cambodia. The predominant doctrinal strain of this transmission was Theravāda/Nikāya 部派 tradition, which bases its teachings on the Pāli Canon 南傳大藏經.

❖ ***Sutta on the Source of the Vinaya*** 毘尼母經: The Pinimu jing. (Skt. *Vinaya-mātikā*) 8 fasc., K 939, T 1463; also referred to as Pinimu lun 毘尼母論 and Mulun 母論. Translator unknown. Listed in the Qin lu 秦録 (350–431).1

Nanjō 1138; Ono. 9:144a. Although this work is called a sutta, it is actually an early Chinese translation of a commentary vinaya texts. The content focuses on the differences between the Ten Recitations Vinaya 十誦律 and the Four Part Vinaya 四分律. The text also discusses the doctrine that the self is empty but phenomena exist 我空法有, which suggests Sarvâstivādin influence.

❖ **Ten precepts** 十戒: These are also the ten basic precepts for *Bhikkhus* and *Bhikkhunīs* in Theravāda and Nikāya Buddhism. Also known as the 沙彌十戒 or 沙彌戒. The first five of these (五戒) are also observed by lay practitioners:

1. not killing 不殺生 pāṇātipātāveramaṇi;
2. not stealing 不偷盜 adinnādānāver;
3. no improper sexual behavior (such as adultery, etc.) 不邪婬;
4. no false speech 不妄語 musāvādāver;
5. no consumption of alcohol 不飲酒;
6. not eating after noon 不非時食 vikāla-bhojanāver;
7. not watching dancing, singing and shows 不歌舞觀聽;
8. not adorning oneself with garlands, perfumes and ointments 不塗飾香鬘;

9. not using a high bed 不坐高廣大牀 uccāsayanā-mahāsayanā;

10. not receiving gold and silver 不蓄金銀寶

❖ **Theravāda (Buddhism)** 上座部(佛教): The Chinese translation of the Sanskrit Sthaviravāda and Pāli Theravāda. One of the earliest schools of Buddhism that developed in India during the century subsequent to the passing away of the Buddha, initially distinguished from the Mahāsāṃghika 大衆部. The name of the school implies the meaning of 'those supporting the teachings of the elders' which means that this was a school that had conservative tendencies—an attempt to conserve the original teachings of the Buddha. At first the Sthaviras and Mahāsāṃghikas were not considered to be different schools, the former merely representing the intimate and older disciples of Sakyamuni and the latter being the rest. It is said that a century later under Mahādeva 大天 a difference of opinion arose regarding interpretations of the Vinaya 律 and other matters, with the more liberal Mahāsāṃghika school espousing a revisionist approach to the Buddhist doctrine. Descendants of the Sthaviras continue to be active to the present in Southeast Asian countries such as Sri Lanka, Myanmar, Thailand and Cambodia. Later schools of Mahāyāna Buddhism categorized the Theravāda 上座部 and other Nikāya schools as being lesser vehicle, or Hīnayāna 小乘.

* **Three refuges** 三歸依: The three surrenders to, or 'formulas of refuge' in, the three treasures 三寶, i.e. to the Buddha 佛, the *Dhamma* 法, the *saṅgha* 僧. All Buddhists, whether monk or lay practitioners, are to take refuge. Also written as 三歸依 and 三依. The three formulas are 歸依佛 buddhaṃ saraṇaṃ gacchāmi, 歸依法 Dhammaṃ saraṇaṃ gacchāmi, 歸依僧 saṅghaṃ saraṇaṃ gacchāmi; these are to be repeated three times. It is 'the most primitive formula fidei of the early Buddhists.'

* **Three treasures** 三寶: Three precious things; three objects of veneration 三尊 (*tiratna*). The various scriptures and treatises in the Buddhist canon contain an extensive array of interpretations regarding the precise connotations of these three, both in terms of the meaning of the term itself, and in terms of their relationship to each other. The basic set of three are (1)

the Buddha 佛; (2) the *Dhamma* (Buddhist teachings) 法, and (3) the *Saṅgha* (community of monks and nuns) 僧.

❖ **Twelve links of dependent arising** 十二緣起: When inquiring into what it is that gives rise to human suffering, the Buddha found it to be a continuum of twelve phases of conditioning in a regular order. These twelve links of conditioned existence are:

1. (avijjā 無明) *nescience (ignorance, unenlightenment)* ;

2.(*saṅkhāra* 行), action-intentions; action, activity, conception, karmicpredispositions

3. (*viññāṇa* 識) consciousness;

4. (*nāma-rūpa* 名色) name and form;

5. (*saḷāyatana* 六處) the six-fold sphere of sense contact;

6. (*phassa* 觸) contact;

7. (*vedanā* 受) sensation, feeling;

8. (*taṇhā* 愛) thirst, desire, craving;

9. (*upādāna* 取) grasping, appropriation;

10. (*bhāva* 有) becoming, being, existing;

11. (*jāti* 生) birth;

12. (*jarāmaraṇa* 老死) old age and death (impermanence).

In this order, the prior situation is the condition for the arising of the next situation. Also, in the same order, if the prior condition is extinguished, the next condition is extinguished. The classical formula reads "By reason of nescience dispositions; by reason of dispositions consciousness," etc.

A further application of the twelve nidānas is made in regard to their causation of rebirth:

(1) nescience, as inherited affliction from the beginn-
    ingless past;

(2) *kamma*, good and evil, of past lives;

(3) conception as a form of perception;

(4) *nāma-rūpa*, or body and mind evolving(in the womb);

(5) the six organs on the verge of birth;

(6) childhood whose intelligence is limited to sparśa,
    contact or touch;

(7) receptivity or budding intelligence and discrimination
    from 6 or 7 years;

(8) thirst, desire, or love, age of puberty;

(9) the urge of sensuous existence;

(10) forming the substance, *bhāva*, of future *kamma*;

(11) the completed *kamma* ready for rebirth;

(12) old age and death. The two first are associated

with the previous life, the other ten with the present. The theory is equally applicable to all realms of reincarnation. The twelve links are also represented in a chart, at the center of which are the serpent (anger), boar(nescience, or stupidity), and dove (lust) representing the fundamental sins. Each catches the other by the tail, typifying the train of sins producing the wheel of life.

In another circle the twelve links are represented as follows:

(1) nescience, a blind woman;

(2) action, a potter at work, or man gathering fruit;

(3) consciousness, a restless monkey;

(4) name and form, a boat;

(5) sense organs, a house;

(6) contact, a man and woman sitting together;

(7) sensation, a man pierced by an arrow;

(8) desire, a man drinking wine;

(9) craving, a couple in union;

(10) existence through childbirth;

(11) birth, a man carrying a corpse;

(12) disease, old age, death, an old woman leaning on a stick.

An alternative rendering of 十二因緣.

❖ *Verses of the Elder Nuns* 長老尼偈: A collection of 522 religious poems by elder nuns of the Buddhist monastic order. (Pāli. Therī-gāthā) transliterated as 涕利伽陀. A part of the Pāli *Khuddaka-nikāya* 小部經.

❖ **Vimalakīrti-nirdeśa-sūtra** 維摩經: This scripture is considered one of the most profound, as well as literarily excellent of the Indian Mahāyāna suttas. The sutta expounds the deeper principle of Mahāyāna as opposed to lesser vehicle teachings, focusing on the explication of the meaning of nonduality. A significant aspect of the scripture is the fact that it is a teaching addressed to high-ranking Buddhist disciples through the mouth of the layman bodhisatta Vimalakīrti, who expounds the doctrine of emptiness in depth, eventually resorting to silence.

❖ **Vinaya of the Four Categories** 四分律: The influential Vinaya text transmitted from the Dhammagupta school 法藏部. Translated by Buddhayaśas 佛陀耶舍 (408–413 CE) and Fonian 竺佛念 (412–413 CE). Related Vinaya texts include T 1429–1434. Along with the Sarvâstivāda vinaya 十誦律 (T 1435), the Mahīśāsaka Vinaya 五分律

(T 1421) and the Mahāsāṃghika Vinaya 摩訶僧祇律 (T 1425), one of the four major Vinaya works transmitted to East Asia. This work investigates the origins and causes by which the *pātimokkha* 波羅提木叉 enumerate the offenses of the precepts of the *Bhikkhus* and *Bhikkhunīs*—especially distinguishing the reasons for the lightness and heaviness of punishments. There is also detailed explanation consisting of two parts (*khandhaka*) dealing with various concrete regulations concerning activities of everyday life, of ceremonies, rules of behavior. These are divided along the lines of stopping of evil 止惡 and the cultivation of goodness 作善. These explanations are given in four parts, from which the text derives its name.

1. For the monks: the four grave offenses 四波羅夷法, the thirteen crimes against the *saṅgha* 十三僧殘, the two indeterminates 二不定法, the thirty offenses requiring expatiation and forfeiture 三十捨墮法, the ninety offenses requiring expatiation 九十單墮法, the four offenses regarding meals 四提舍尼法, the hundred admonishments for polishing conduct 衆學法, and the seven methods for resolving disputes 七滅諍法.

2. For the nuns: the eight grave offenses (尼律)八波羅夷
法, the seventeen crimes against the *sangha* (尼律)
十七僧殘法, the thirty offenses requiring expatiation
and forfeiture (尼律)三十捨墮法, the 178 offenses
requiring only expatiation (尼律)百七十八單墮法, the
eight offenses regarding meals (尼律)八提舍尼法, the
hundred methods of polishing behavior (尼律)百衆學
法, the seven methods of resolving disputes (尼律)七
滅諍法. From here, the text is divided into explanatory
sections, called *khandhaka* 犍度. These sections
deal with the following items, extending through
the remaining sections of the text: ordination 受戒,
teaching the precepts 說戒, and retreats 安居.

3. The third part continues with these explanations,
including teachings regarding self-indulgence 自
恣, regulations on the use of leather goods 皮革,
clothing 衣, medicines 藥, handling of clothing during
the retreat 迦締那衣, struggles between persons 拘睒
彌, admonitions of improper behavior 瞻波, rebuking
quarrelsome monks 呵責, correction of minor crimes
人, remedies for those who conceal their crimes 覆
藏, dealing with offenses not treated at the *uposatha*

遮, the destruction of the *sangha* 破僧, resolution of disputes 滅諍, reception of the nuns precepts 比丘尼, ritual performances 法

4. residence, boarding, bedding, etc. 房舍, miscellany 雜 (tools, implements and so forth), precepts theory 集法 (history of the development of the precepts and so forth), treatment of special occurrences 調部, technical terminology 毘尼增一. Although the number of precepts are generally explained to be 250 for monks in Buddhism, it is actually only this text that teaches that number—along with 348 for nuns.

❖ **Vipassanā** 觀: Insight. 'Analytical meditation'. Examination (Skt. *vipaśyanā*) as contrasted to 'concentration meditation' *samatha*; 止, 定). Investigation; to analyze or investigate the principle of things with wisdom. Using previously-cultivated concentration to investigate a Buddhist truth, such as dependent arising or emptiness. To see things as they really are. To contemplate and mentally enter into truth; to consider illusion and discern illusion, or discern the seeming from the real. Sometimes used as a general term for 'meditation' or 'contemplation,' but also used with specific technical connotations. 覺 is defined as awakening, or awareness, 觀 as examination or study.

❖ **Voice-hearer** 聲聞: Originally, a direct disciple of the Buddha (who heard his voice). (Tib. nyan thos) In later Mahāyāna texts, a technical term with somewhat negative connotations. While *sāvaka* are disciplined monk-practitioners who contemplate the principle of the four noble truths for the purpose of the attainment of *arahant*-ship 阿羅漢, and thus eventually *Nibbāna*, they are also considered along with the Pacceka-Buddha 辟支佛, to be a practitioner of the two lesser vehicles (二乘, 小乘), inferior in insight and compassion to the bodhisatta 菩薩. This is because their practice is said to be self-centered, focusing on their own salvation 自 利, a selfishness that is made possible by their lack of recognition of the emptiness of all objective phenomena 法空.

❖ **Wonhyo** 元曉: (617–686) One of the most influential Buddhist thinkers, writers and commentators—not only of the Korean Buddhist tradition— but also in all of East

Asian Buddhist history. With his life spanning the end of the Three Kingdoms period (57–668) and the beginning of the Unified Silla (668–935), Wonhyo played a vital role in the reception and assimilation of the broad range of doctrinal Buddhist streams that flowed into East Asia at the time. While Wonhyo was most interested in, and affected by Tathāgatagarbha 如來藏 and Yogâcāra 唯識 thought, in his extensive scholarly works, delivered mostly in the form of commentaries along with a few treatises, he strove to interpret the entire spectrum of the Mahāyāna Buddhist teachings that were received in East Asia, including such traditions as Pure Land 淨土宗, *Nibbāna* Sutta studies 涅槃宗, *Lotus Sutta* studies, Huayan 華嚴宗, Sanlun 三論宗, Logic 因明, Vinaya studies 戒律, and State Protection. He wrote commentaries on virtually all of the most influential Mahāyāna scriptures, altogether including over eighty works in over two hundred fascicles. Among his most influential works were the commentaries he wrote on the *Awakening of Faith* 大乘起信論, *Nibbāna Sutta* 涅槃經 and *Vajrasamādhi Sutta* 金剛三昧經. These were treated with utmost respect by leading Buddhist scholars in China and Japan, and his work on the *Awakening of Faith* served to help in establishing that text as one of the most influential in East Asia. Wonhyo spent the earlier part of his career as a monk, but later left the priesthood to spread the buddha-*Dhamma* as a layman. Recorded as having led a colorful and unfettered lifestyle during this period, Wonhyo ended up becoming somewhat of a folk hero in Korea. He was a colleague and friend of the influential Silla Hwaeom 華嚴 scholar Uisang 義湘, and it can be said that Wonhyo's scholarly efforts at elucidating Tathāgatagarbha doctrines contributed to Uisang's efforts in establishing Hwaeom as a dominant stream of doctrinal thought on the Korean peninsula.

❖ **Wonhyo's Thought**: Wonhyo, without being affiliated with any particular school or doctrinal tradition, applied himself to the explication of all the major Mahāyāna source texts that were available at the time, and in doing so brought about a major impact on East Asian Buddhism. He is cited extensively, and his interpretations of the texts from this broad range of traditions are taken seriously in subsequent commentarial works in China, Korea, and Japan. The key terms that have been applied in modern times to characterize his overall approach as seen in his writings are those of 'harmonization of disputes' (*hwajaeng*; 和諍) and interpenetrated Buddhism (*tong bulgyo*; 通佛教).

As a methodological approach, *hwajaeng* 和諍 refers to Wonhyo's relentless pursuit of ostensibly variant or conflicting Buddhist doctrinal or hermeneutical positions, investigating them exhaustively until identifying the precise point at which their variance occurs, and then showing how differences in fundamental background, motivation, or sectarian bias on the part of the proponent of that particular doctrinal position lead to the production of his own approach, which stands in conflict with those of other scholars. Wonhyo engages in this exercise repeatedly, in every extant commentary, in every essay and treatise—to an extent not seen in the works of any other East Asian exegete. In this manner, his approach differs somewhat from some of his contemporary scriptural commentators in China, in that in his works we do not see the application of the practice of doctrinal classification (*pangyo* 判教).13

One of most concentrated and sustained examples of this ecumenical approach can be seen in Wonhyo's

Simmun hwajaeng non (十門和諍論; Ten Approaches to the Reconciliation of Doctrinal Disputes), for which we unfortunately only have fragments from the beginning portion. This is one of Wonhyo's very few works that is not a commentary, and is not composed for the purpose of resolving a singular doctrinal theme. It is rather a methodological exercise that selectively utilizes Mādhyamika and Dignāgan logic, interwoven with the motifs of the major Mahāyāna scriptures, including *the Lotus Sutta, Nibbāna Sutta, Yogâcārabhūmi-śāstra, Paññāpāramitā Sutta*, and so on. As in his other works, Wonhyo's aim is to work through ostensibly conflicting doctrinal problems using rigorous logic to clarify their content, reveal their underpinnings, and ultimately demonstrate their compatibility with the Mahāyāna Buddhist system as a whole. At the same time, while fully investigating all the disputes and pending issues that appeared between schools and their scriptures and treatises, as well as differences in current trends of thought, Wonhyo used the discussion of these variant positions to clearly establish his own position. Wonhyo's overriding concern with the harmonization of disputes is seen not only in this text, but pervades every corner of his extant writings.

The Korean Culture Series Published by the International Cultural Foundation

Korean Culture Series 1

1. *Humor in Korean Literature*
2. *Upper Class Culture in Joseon-Dynasty Korea*
3. *Buddhist Culture in Korea*
4. *Folklore Culture in Korea*
5. *Legal System of Korea*
6. *Korean Society*
7. *Korean Folk Tales*
8. *Economic Life in Korea*
9. *Customs and Manners in Korea*
10. *Korean Thought*

Korean Culture Series (Special Issues)

1. *General Questions on Korean Culture*
2. *Koreans and Korean Culture*

Korean Culture Series II

1. *Root of Korean Culture*
2. *Culture of Korean Shamanism*
3. *The King's Secret Emissary in the Joseon Dynasty*
4. *Korean Geomancy (Korean feng-shui, pronounced*

poong su in Korean)

5. *Pansori in Korean Culture*
6. *The Culture of Gyu-Bang in Korea (Women's life in Upper Class in Joseon Dynasty)*
7. *Arirang Culture in Korea*
8. *Korean Bhikkunis- Disciples of Buddha (story of Korean Buddhist nuns)*

The International Cultural Foundation

(Gahoedong) #21, 6 Road Buckchonro Jongrogu Seoul, Korea

Board of Directors

Chairman   **Chun, Hong-Duk**

(Former President and CEO of SakeOne, Inc., Former Vice Chancellor of Kimpo College)

Directors   **Kim, Chan-Kyu**

(Honorary President of the Korean Society of International Law)

Cho, Han-Seung

(Ex-A Member of Board of Education of Gyeonggi Do, President of Kimpo Central Loving Campaign)

Han, Sung-Sook

(Ex-Principal of Hongik University Middle School and Girls' High School)

Min, Kyung-Jip

(former executive director of Hite Brewery. a union leader, baekwoo san tourism agicultural cooperative)

Lee, Sang-Sun

(Emeritus Professor of Hanyang University)

Kim, Tae-Jung

(Former Prof. Dept. Tax Accounting of kimpo University)

Auditors　　**Kwak, Jong-Gyoo**

(President and CEO of *Gimpo Journal*)

Paik, Choo-Hye

(Former Executive Officer of The Korean Nutrition Society)

Director of Operation   Kim, Eui-Han
(Chief of Administration of Tongjin Middle School. Ex-Chief of The Develop Division of Kimpo College)

Advertising Director   Jeon, Hyeong-Ki
(Dean of life long Education institut in Kimpo College)